Published to accompany an exhibition by
Sam Fogg Ltd
15D Clifford Street, London W1S 4JZ
www.samfogg.com

The exhibition held at
Luhring Augustine
531 West 24th Street, New York, NY 10011
21 January–12 March 2022
www.luhringaugustine.com

We wish to thank the teams at Sam Fogg and Luhring Augustine for their assistance with this project. Our sincerest thanks also go out to Debra Noel Adams, Elisabeth Banfield, Lauren Batt, Robert Bork, Stephanie Buck, Erik Dop, Alexandra Gajewski, Alessandro Grandolfo, Ketty Gottardo, Gareth Harris, Jack Hartnell, Hanns Hubach, Ethan Matt Kavaler, Armin Kunz, Charles T. Little, Mauro Minardi, Holger Nordmann, Joanna Olchawa, Zoë Opačić, Stefan Roller, Diana Scarisbrick, Peter Schade and Achim Timmermann, for generously sharing their expertise.

AUTHORS
Matthew Reeves & Jana Gajdošová

DESIGN
Richard Ardagh Studio

PHOTOGRAPHY
William Fulton and Barney Hindle

PRE-PRESS
DawkinsColour

PRINTING
Park Communications

Frontispiece:
Detail from cat. 24

THE MEDIEVAL BODY

SAM FOGG

LUHRING
AUGUSTINE

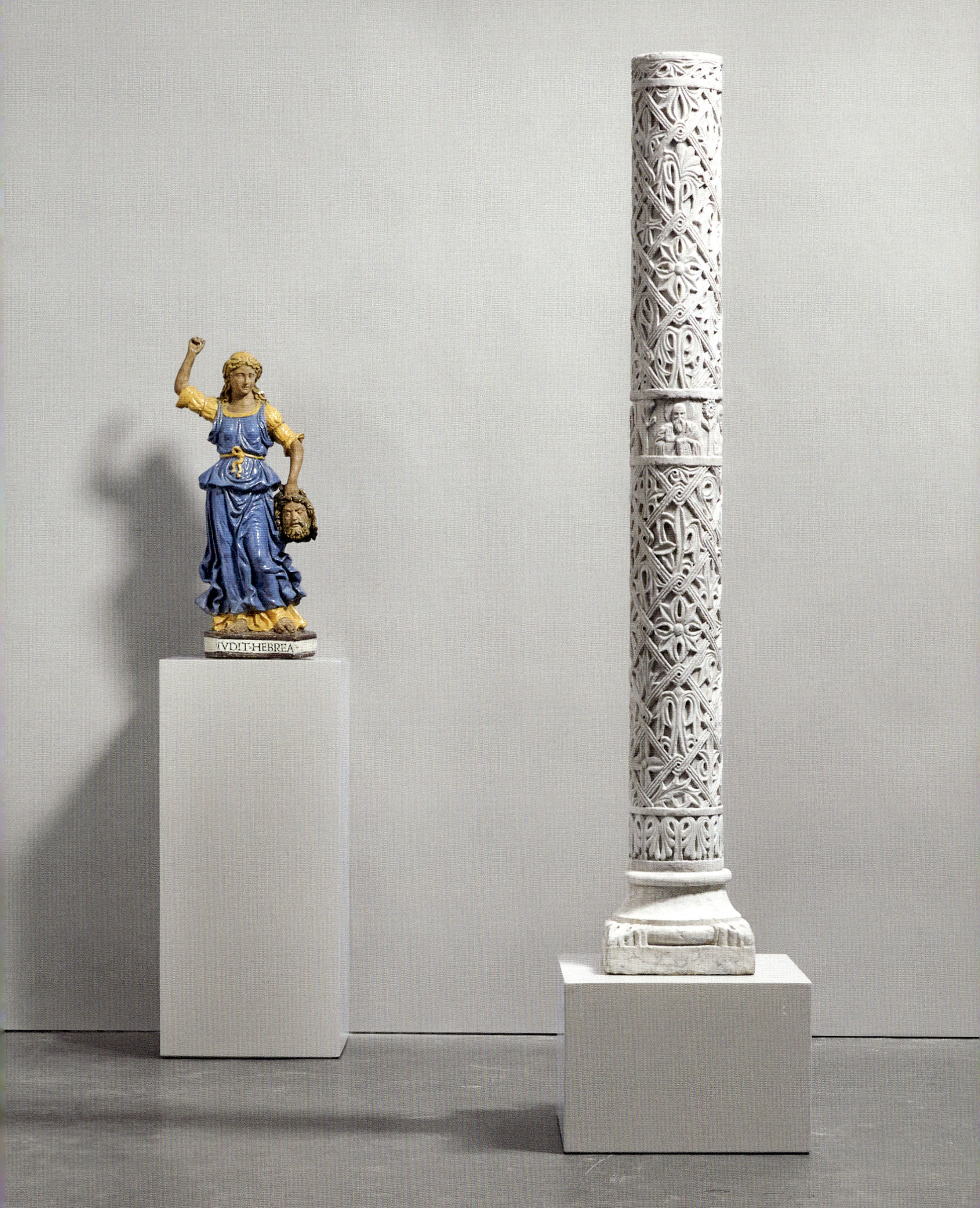

According to medieval thinkers, there was an important duality that existed in every human being – the body and the soul. The body was thought to be flesh, mortal, and corrupt, while the soul was immaterial, perpetual, and linked to God. Some female mystics of the Middle Ages, however, dismissed the separation of body and soul. They viewed the body as an instrument, with which to express the condition of the soul, thus rejecting the notion that the body should be associated exclusively with sin and corruption. Disagreements raged with the body a battleground. The intimate connection between the body and the soul, whether in life or in death, led to the worship of saints' body parts, which were enshrined in lavish reliquaries and chapels in order to underscore their divinity. The churches that housed these sacred bodies were also described with corporeal terms – their cruciform shape mirroring the crucified body of Christ and their interiors often described as the womb of the Virgin Mary.

In art, the medieval body was constantly in flux – trapped between idealism and disfigurement. While the early Middle Ages reserved representations of suffering bodies to the margins of their world, the later Middle Ages displayed wounded bodies in the most central spaces of public life. The crucified body of Christ, wounded and bleeding, assumed the most important position as it was displayed on altars, in processions and on the exteriors of churches. While seemingly gruesome to us today, these images communicated hope and redemption to the medieval viewer by visually linking the physical with the divine.

This exhibition draws on these references, bringing together a group of artworks that tell a unique story about the body as both a physical entity and a recognisable metaphor. Included is a monumental architectural drawing of a sacrament house, attributed to Lorenz Lechler and his workshop, which was designed to ostentatiously display and stage the transubstantiated body of Christ. The Martyrdom of Saint Sebastian by Jörg Lederer gives prominence to the late medieval trend of displaying a suffering human body at the altar, while the Man of Sorrows by the Master of the Holy Kinship communicates the duality of the self, representing a body both dead and alive, human and God. Spanning a period of a thousand years, these works bring us much closer to an understanding that the body in medieval art always had a purpose, despite our own assumptions about its profanity or sanctity.

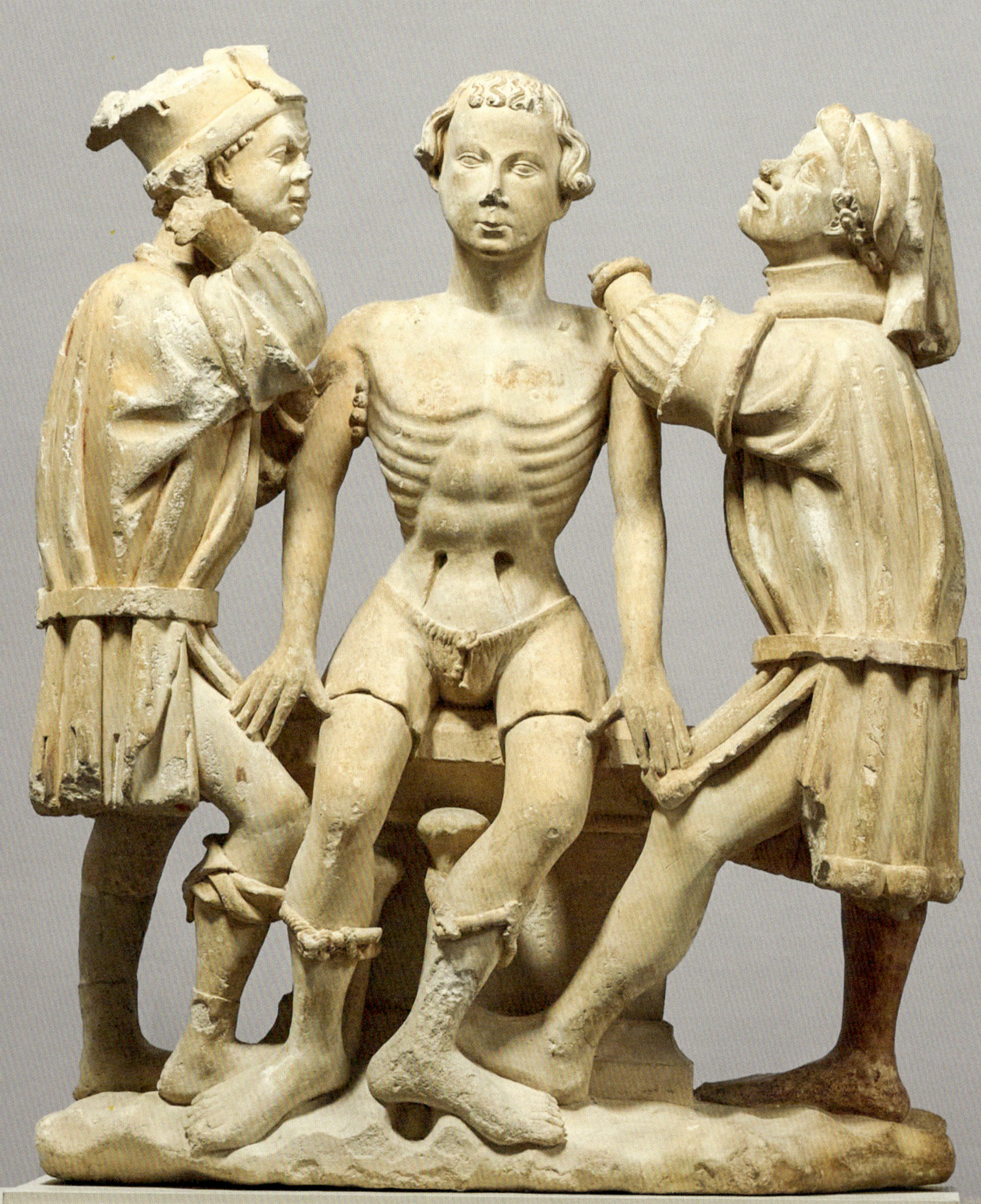

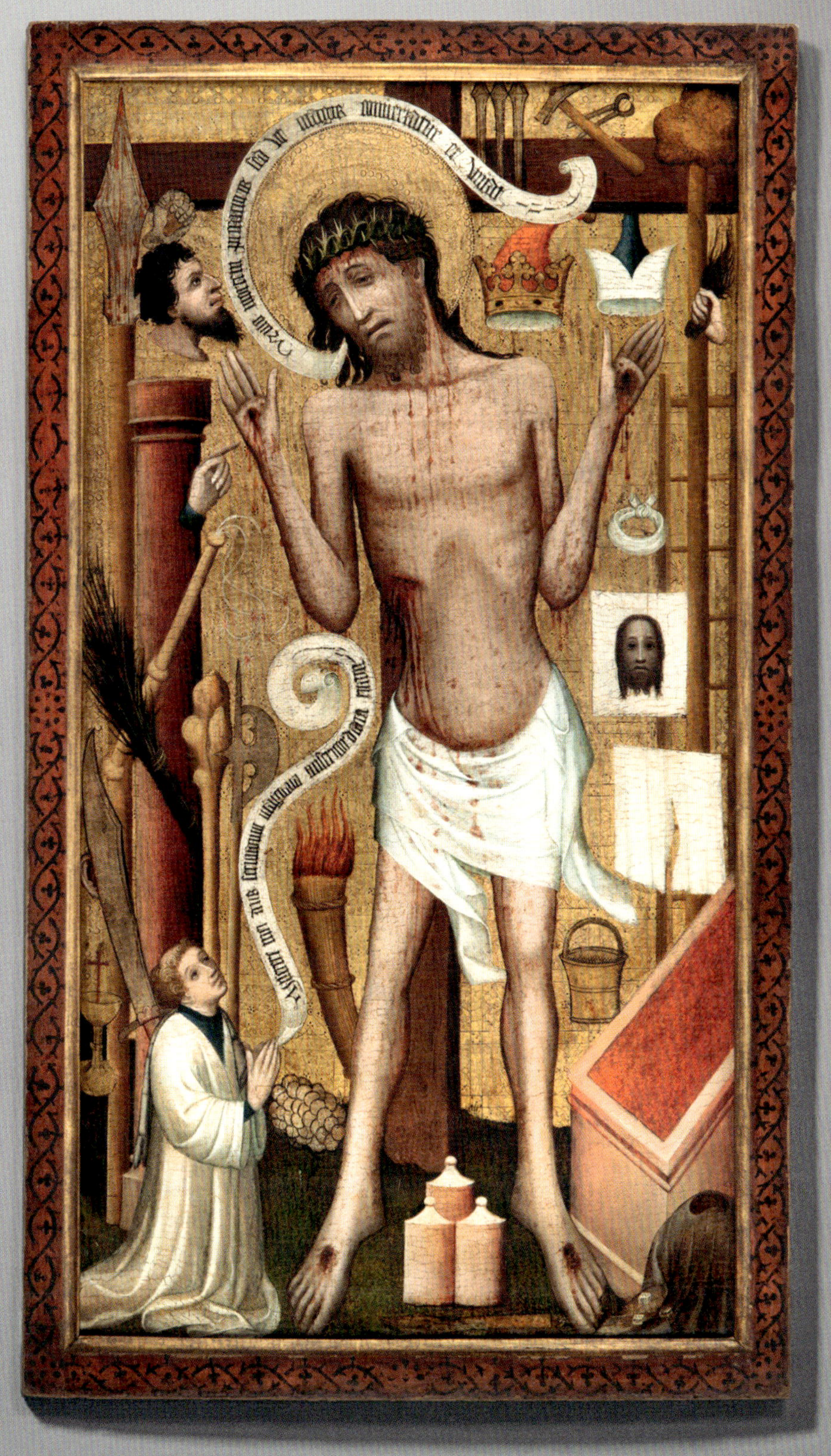

1

A belt buckle inlaid with garnets
Visigothic Spain
c.540–560
13.4 × 6.1 × 2.6 cm / 5.3 × 2.4 × 1 in.
Copper alloy with garnets, glass and cuttlefish
bone supported by gold foils.

PROVENANCE
S. Benzaquen Family, Gibraltar, 1960s;
Private collection, New York, by 1981.

EXHIBITED
Museo National in Mexico City, 1993;
The Meadows Museum, Southern Methodist
University, Dallas, Texas, September 11–
November 9, 1992.

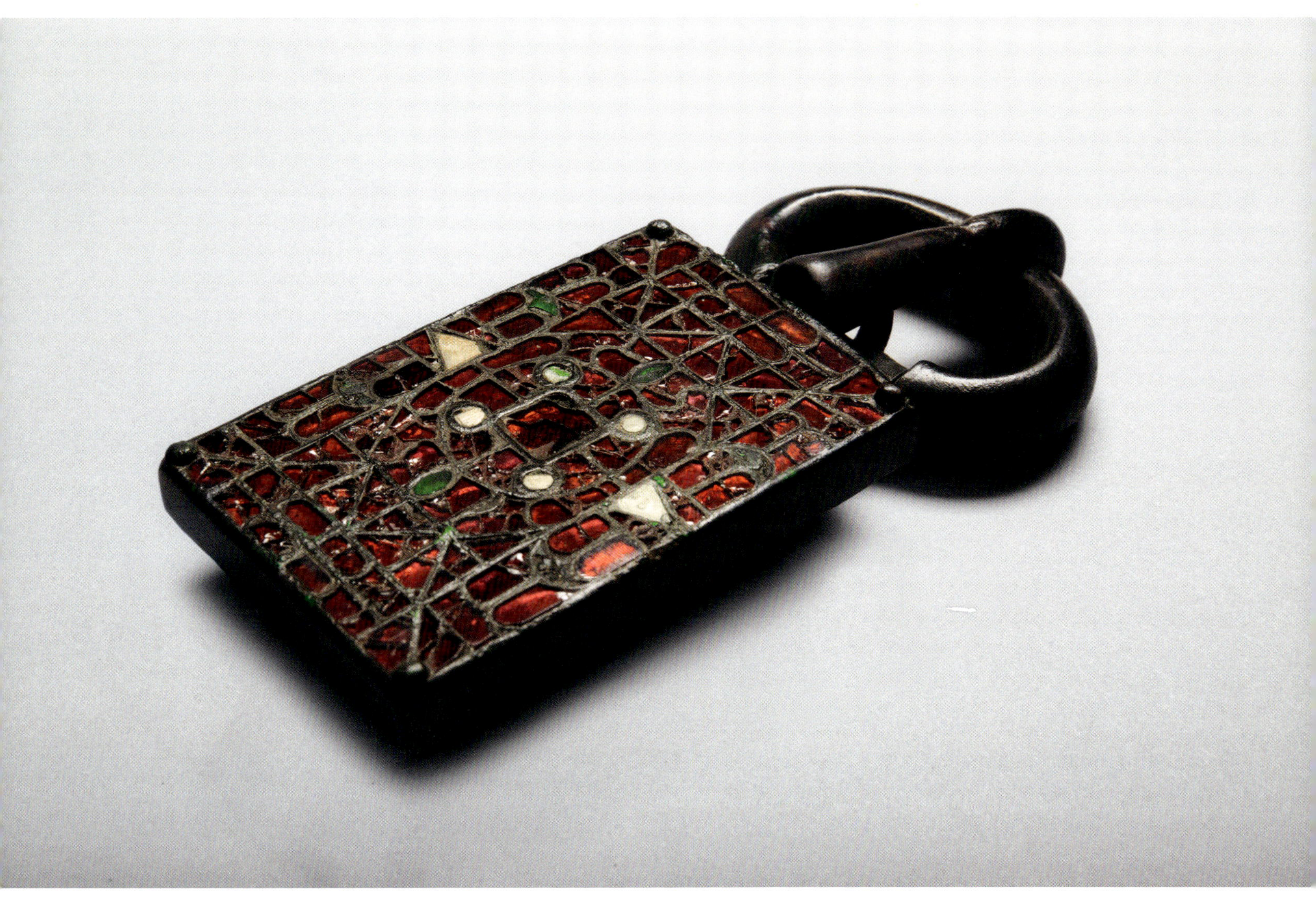

2 **A group of Merovingian brooches from the collection of the Comtesse de Béhague (1870–1939)**
France
*c.*580–600
Garnet brooches: 4 cm / 1.6 in. (diameter) gold, garnet, cement, copper alloy; Disk brooch: 4.4 cm / 1.7 in. (diameter) gold, cement, copper alloy; Bird brooches: 3.3 × 1.8 cm / 1.3 × 0.7 in, silver, gilding, garnet

PROVENANCE
The bird brooches reputedly found at Witternesse, near Saint-Omer, France, in the province of Artois; The whole ensemble brought together by Comtesse Martine-Marie-Octavie Pol de Béhague (1870–1939), Paris; thence by descent to Marquis Jean-Louis Hubert de Ganay (1922–2013); His sale, Antiquités et Objets d'Art: Collection de Martine, Comtesse de Béhague, Provenant de la Succession du Marquis de Ganay, Sotheby's, Monaco, 5 December 1987, lots 41, 49, and 51.

PUBLISHED
Froehner (1905), 20, plate IV; Art in the Dark Ages (1930), 73, 74 plates 25–25, 28 and colour frontispiece; Rupp (1937), plate. 11; Coche de la Ferté (1967), plate 19; Bellanger and Seillier (1982), 87.

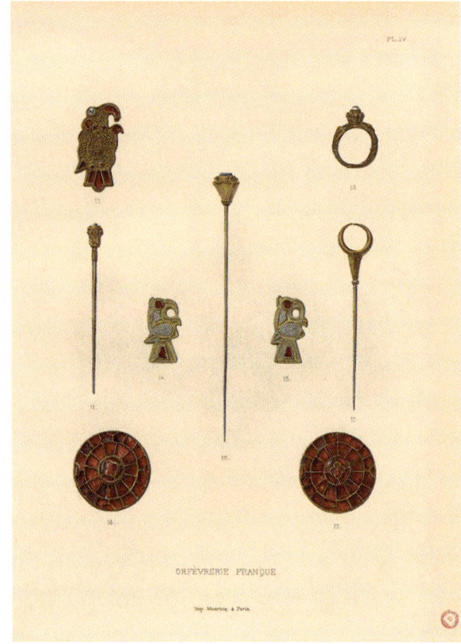

Froehner, 1905 (Plate IV)

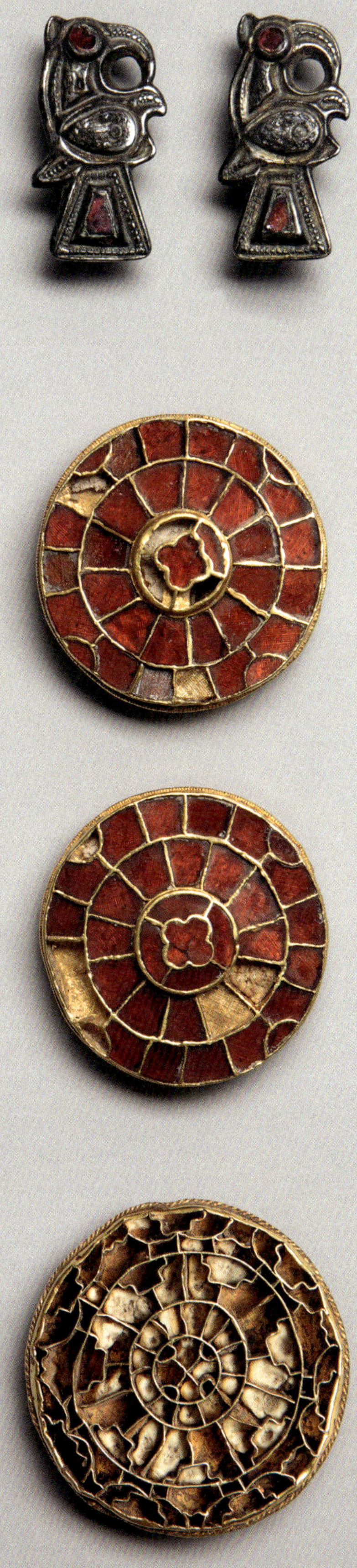

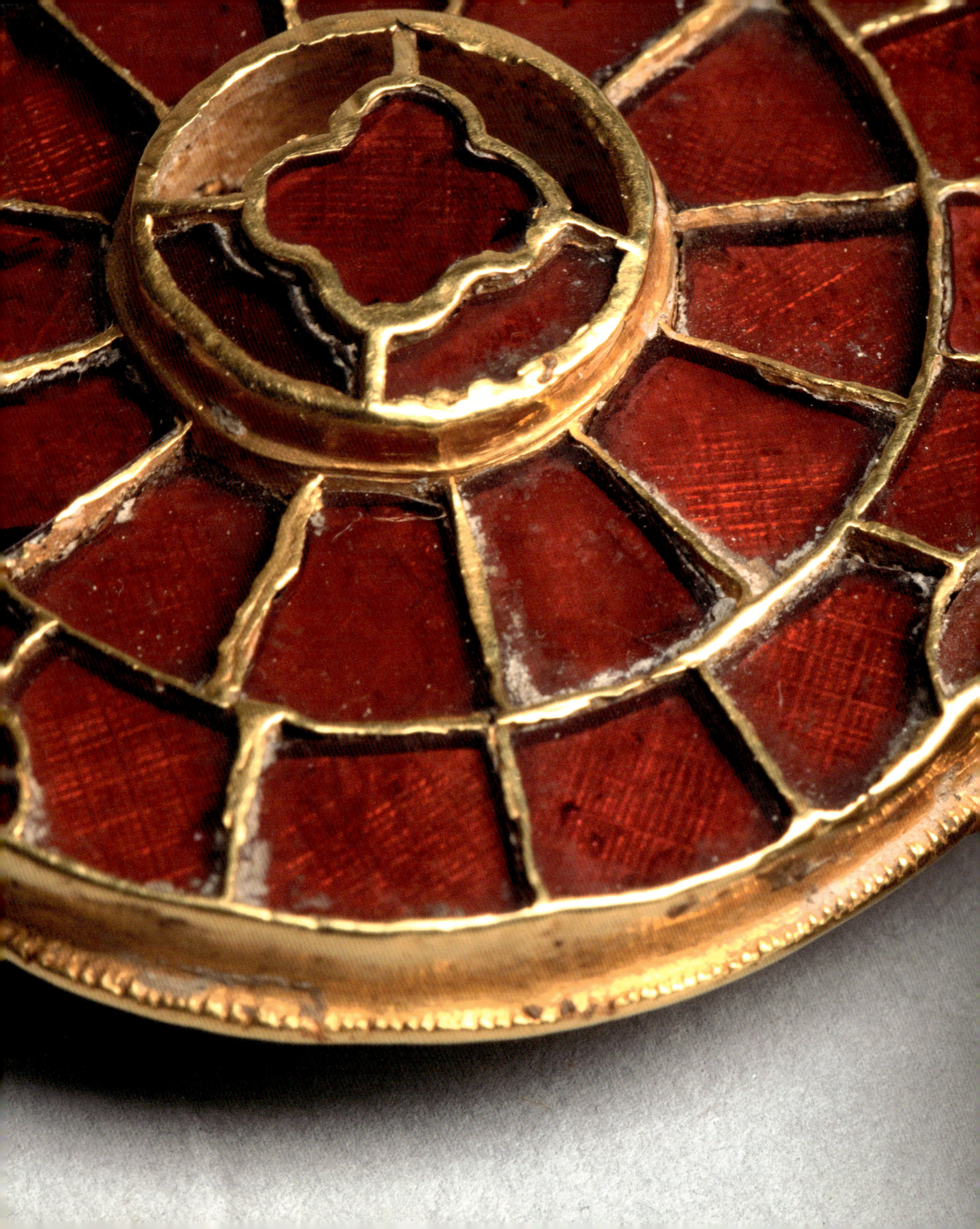

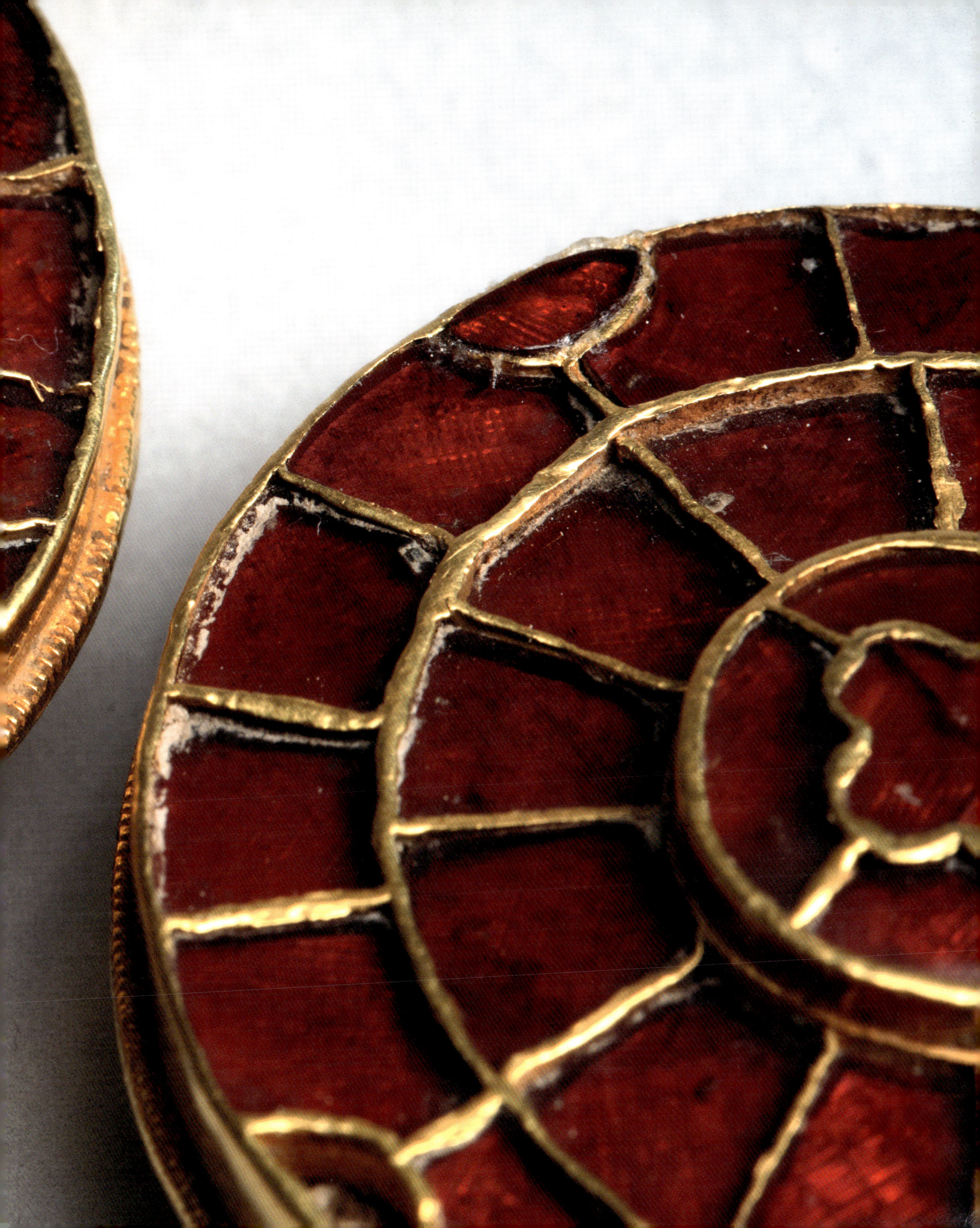

3   A cup with lions' heads emitting flowering rinceaux

England

*c.*1180

7 × 15 × 15 cm / 2.5 × 5.9 × 5.9 in.

Cast, chased, gilded and tooled silver with inlaid blue glass eyes

Collection of Michailas Percovas (1918–2001), Vilnius,
Lithuania, acquired *c.*1970s; by descent to his grandson, Vadim
Lichtenshayn until 2018

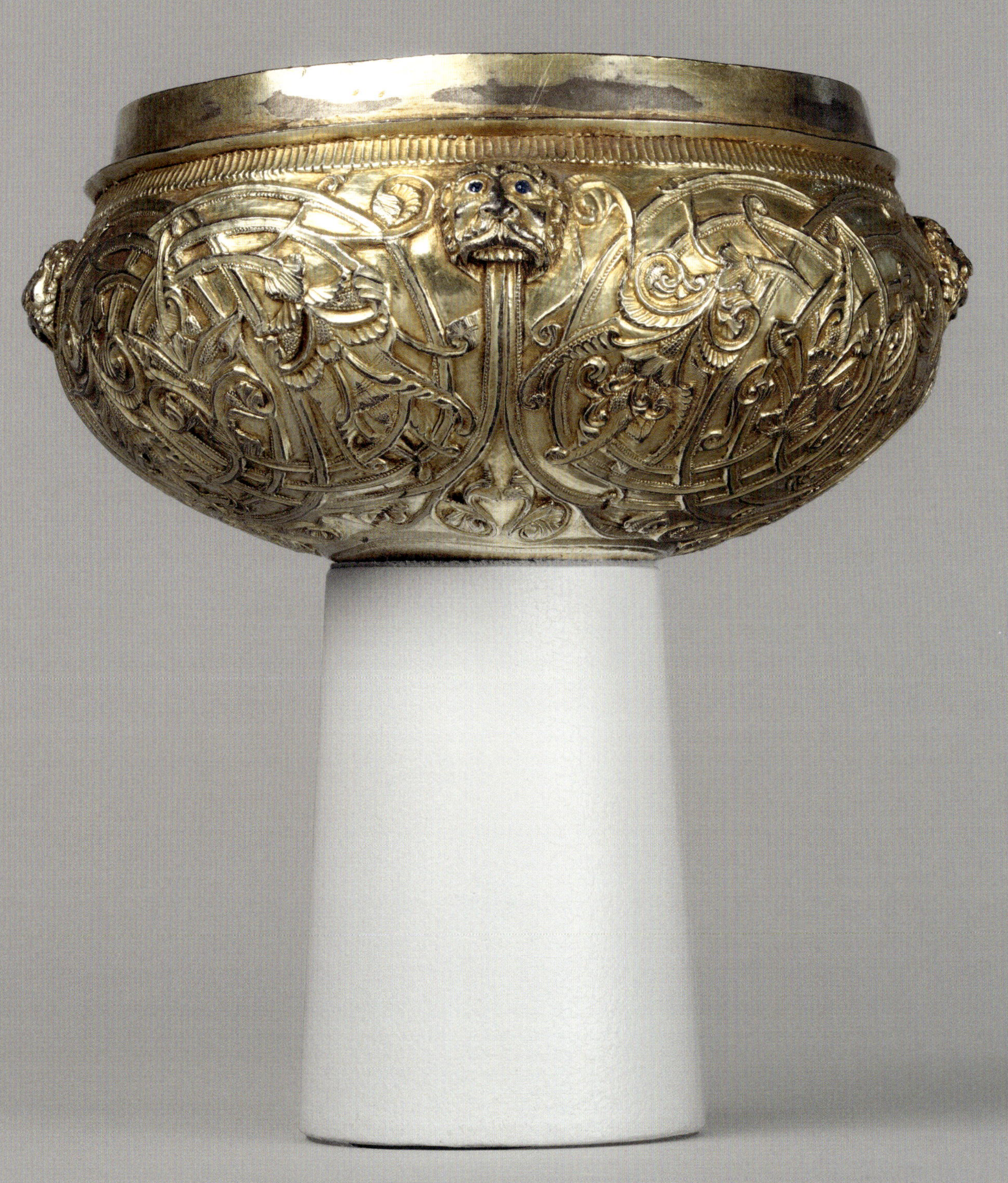

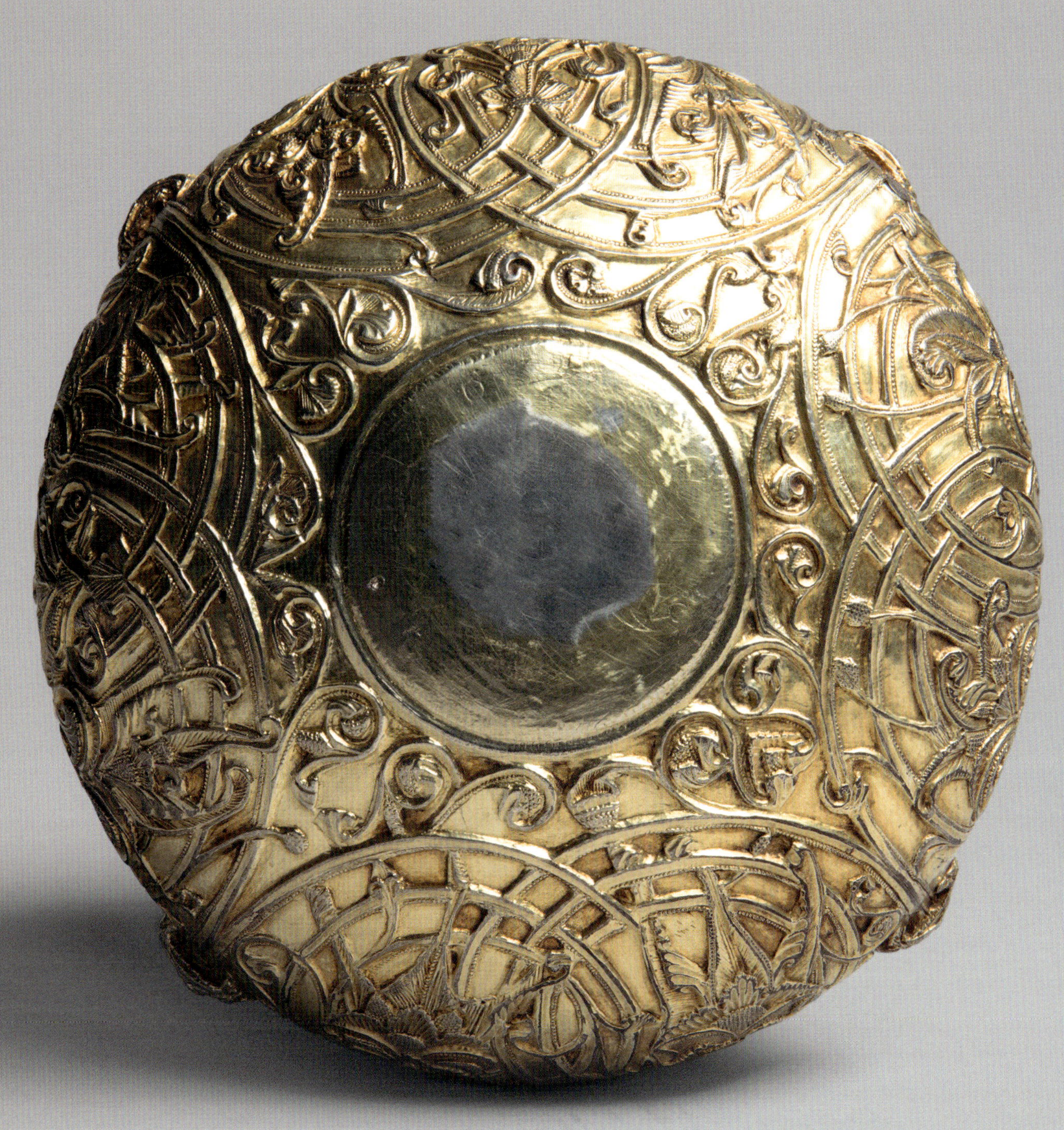

4

Head of an African King
Southern France
*c.*1120–1150
32 × 19 × 22cm / 12.6 × 7.5 × 8.5 in.
Limestone, probably from a church portal

PROVENANCE
Wooden mount by Kichizô Inagaki (1876–1951), the
Paris-based Japanese cabinetmaker (incised with his
monogram); Charles Ratton (1895–1986), Paris, 1949;
Louis Manteau (1886–1968), Brussels, 1957; Gustaaf
Vanderhaegen (1895–1985), Ghent, thence by descent
in his family.

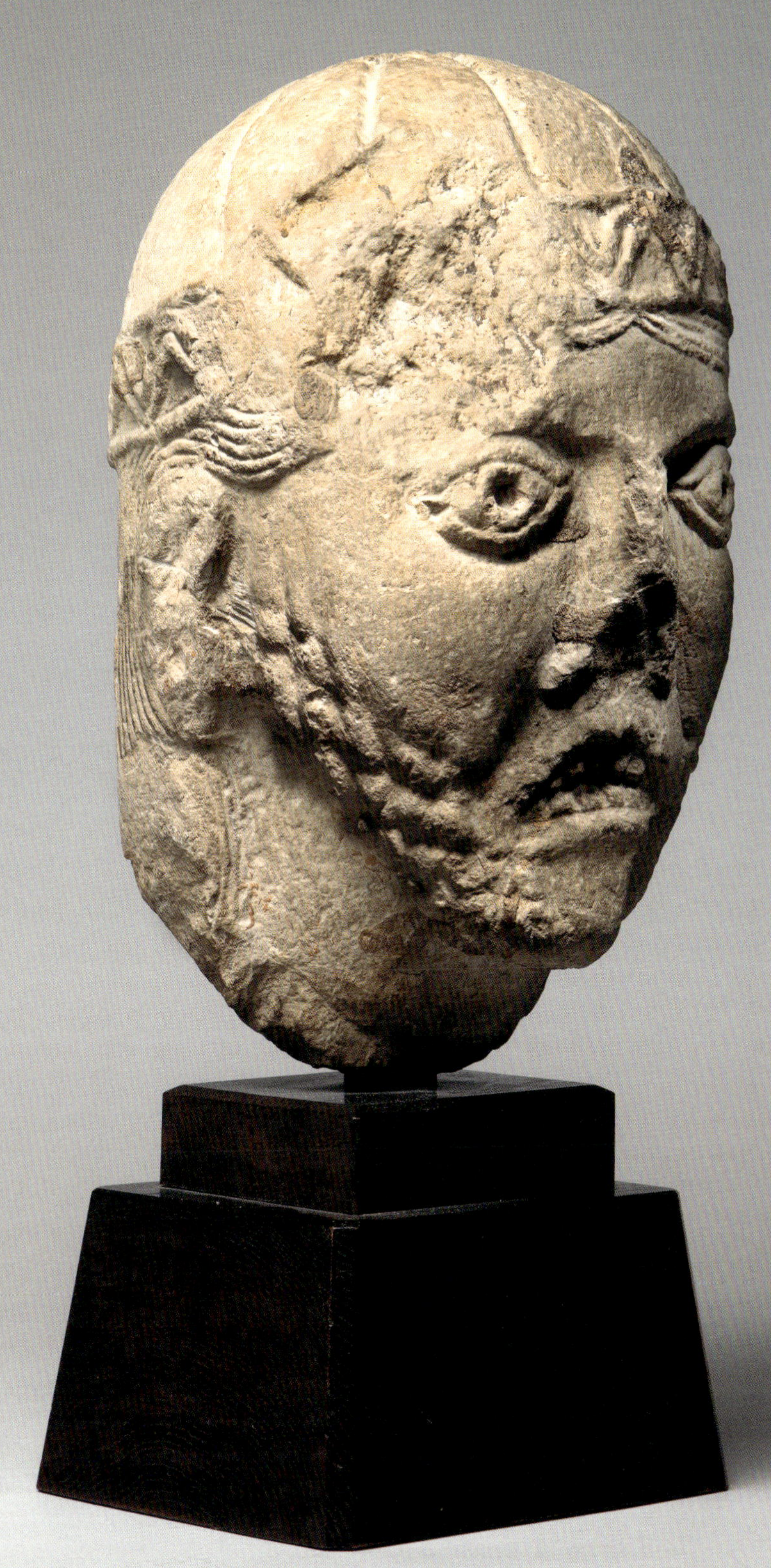

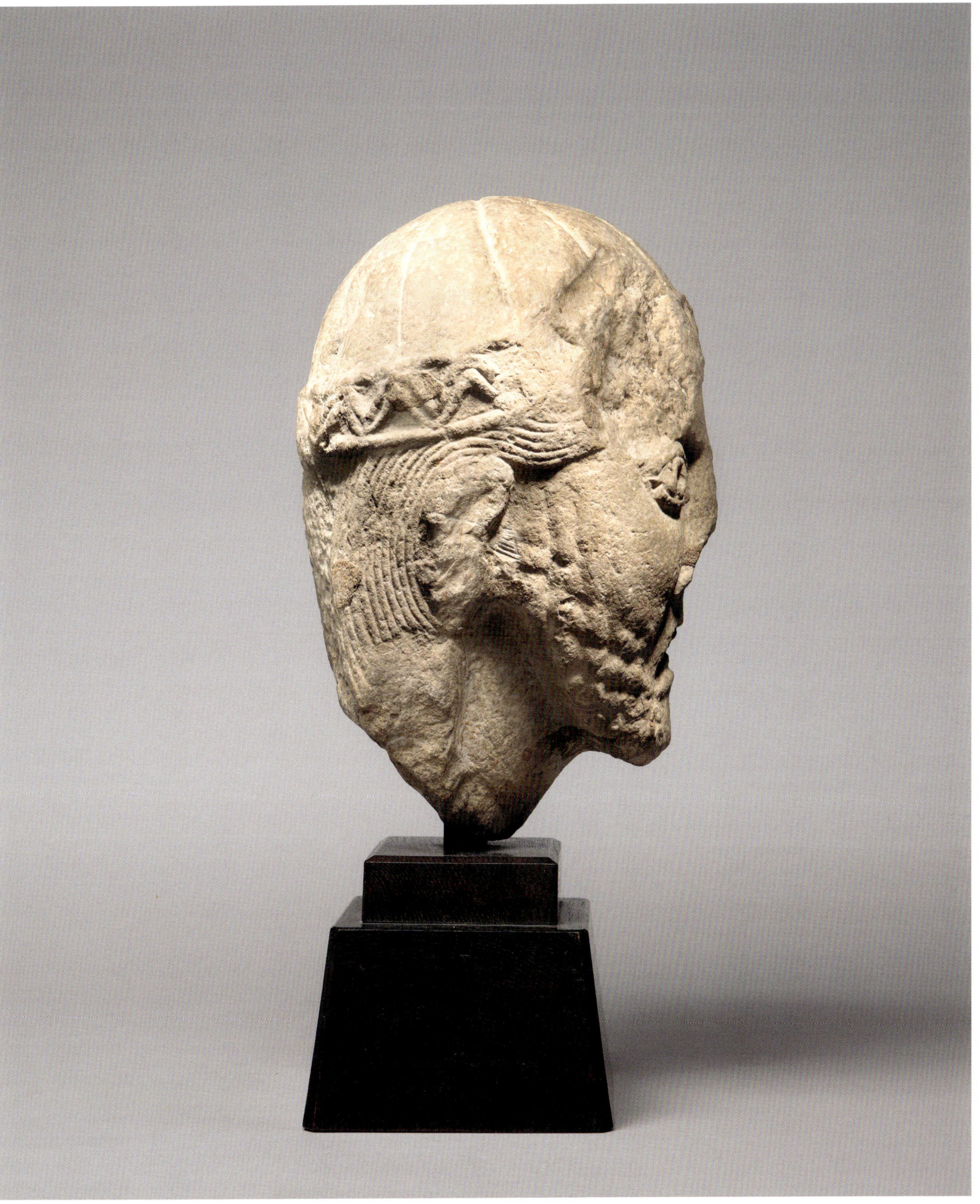

5 **Italo-Byzantine column with acanthus and
images of Apostles**
Italy, Venice (?)
*c.*1180–1200
146 × 24.5 × 24.5 cm / 57.5 × 9.7 × 9.7 in.
Marble, probably from a ciborium

PROVENANCE
Collection of Philip Whiteway, son of Lord Whiteway,
Cimiez, Nice, before 1940.

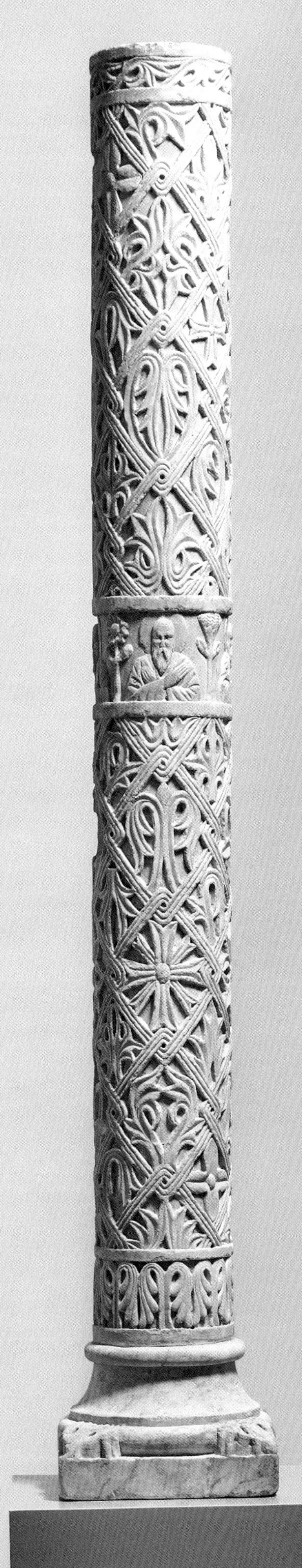

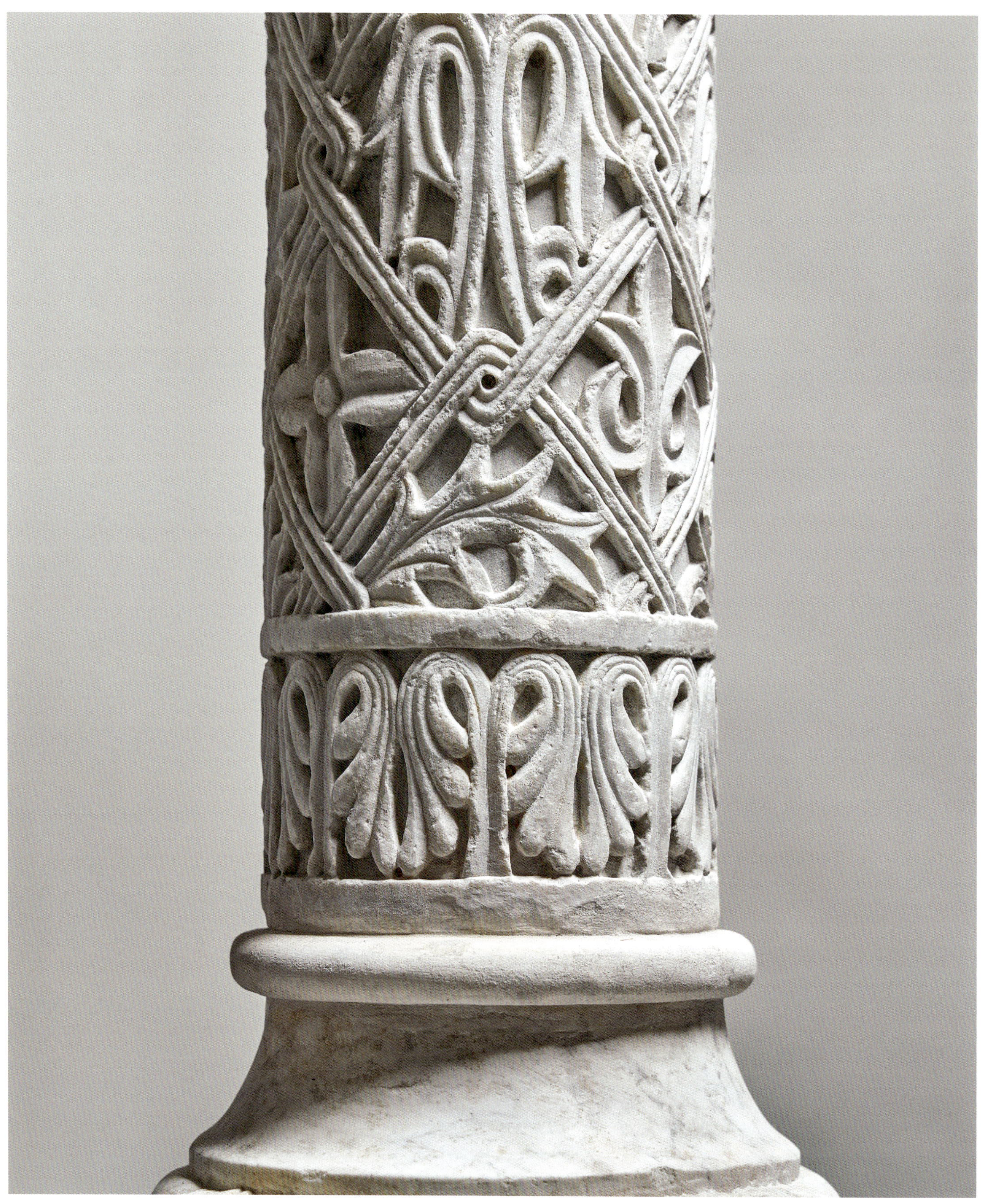

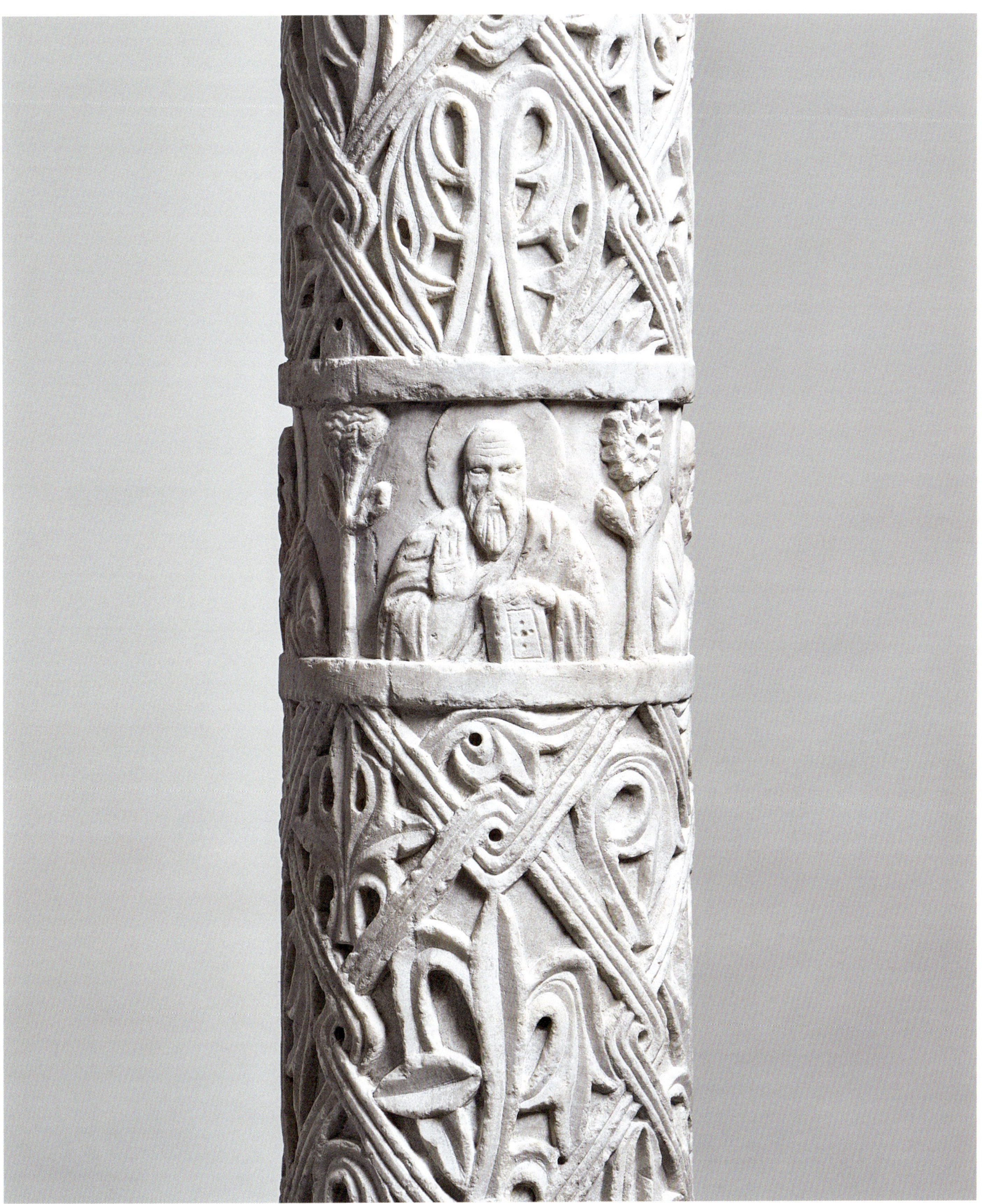

6 A cockerel

Germany, Lower Saxony

*c.*1250–1300

7.7 × 3.2 × 12 cm / 3 × 1.3 × 4.7 in.

Hollow cast, chased and tooled copper alloy,
probably from a candlestick foot

PROVENANCE
Private collection, Massif Central, France.

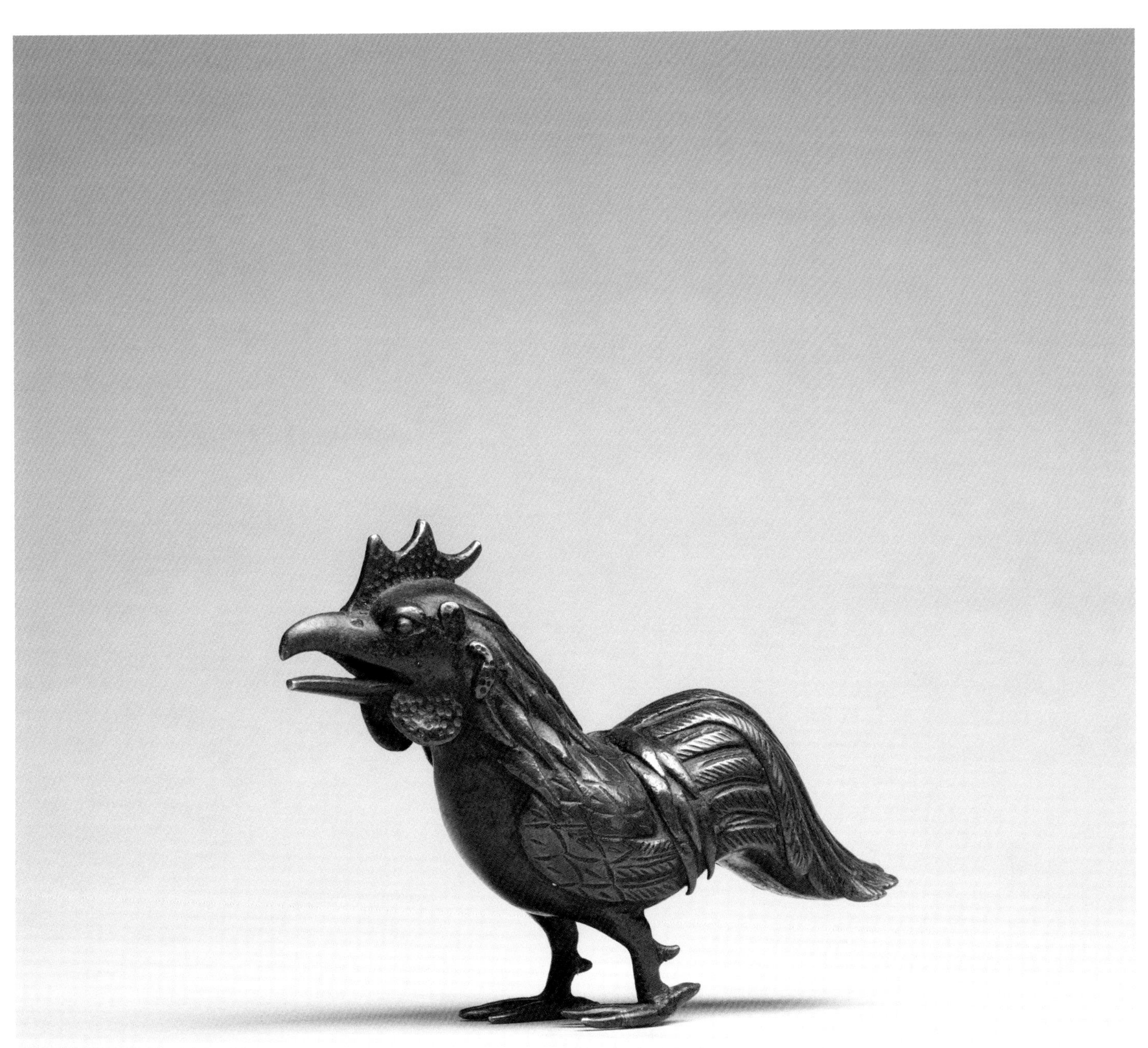

7 Two monumental lions with carving on reverse from a 2nd century Roman triumphal arch

Central Italy

c.1200–1250

58 × 92 × 30cm / 22.8 × 36 × 11.8 in. (lion with carving on reverse); 60 × 85 × 29cm / 23.5 × 33.5 × 11.4 in. (lion with uncarved reverse); metamorphic limestone; originally from the entrance to a church

PROVENANCE

Private collection, Montegiorgio, Ascoli Piceno, Italy, by 1902; Filomeni collection, Ascoli Piceno; Stefano Faenza collection, Ascoli Piceno, acquired from the above in 2003.

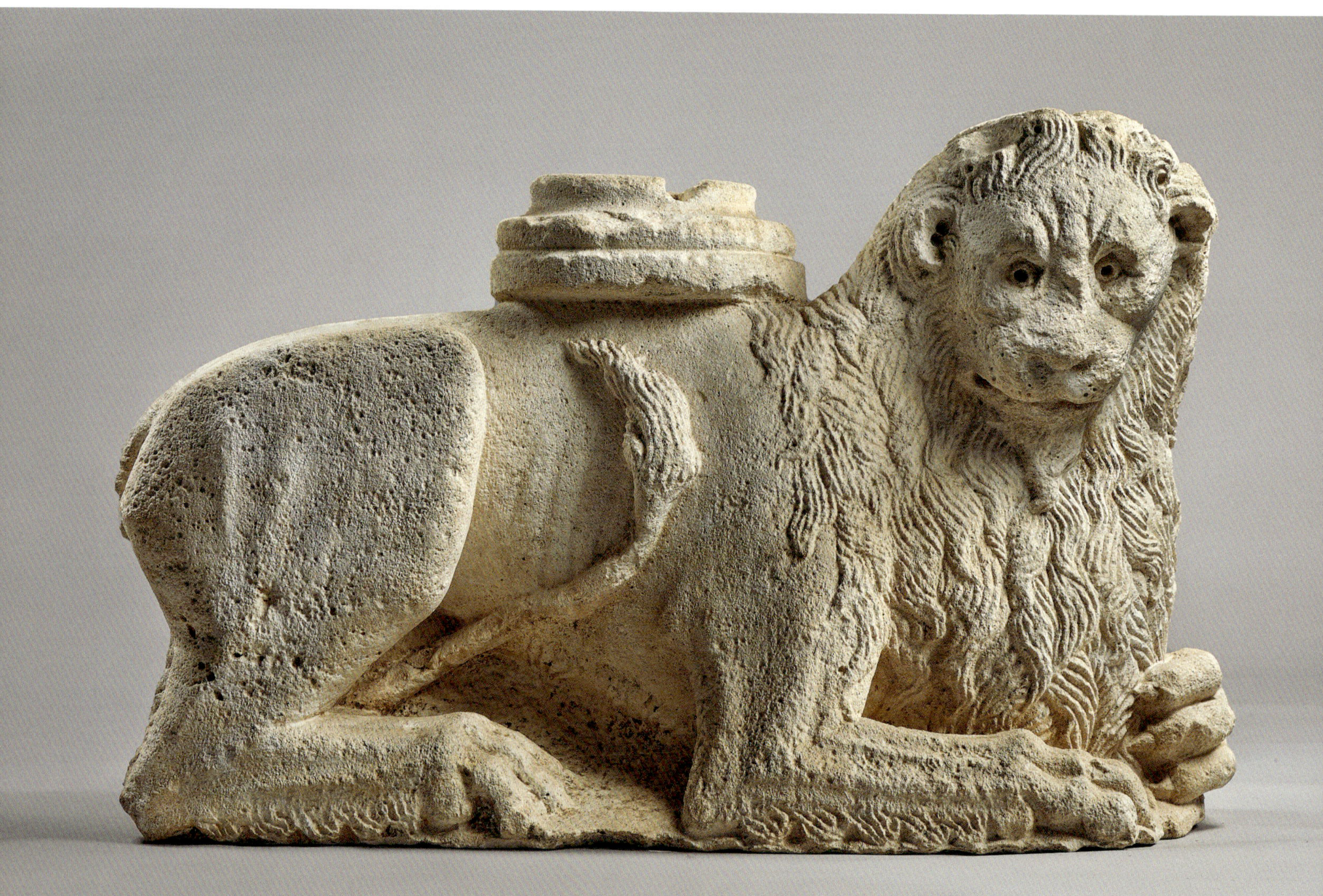

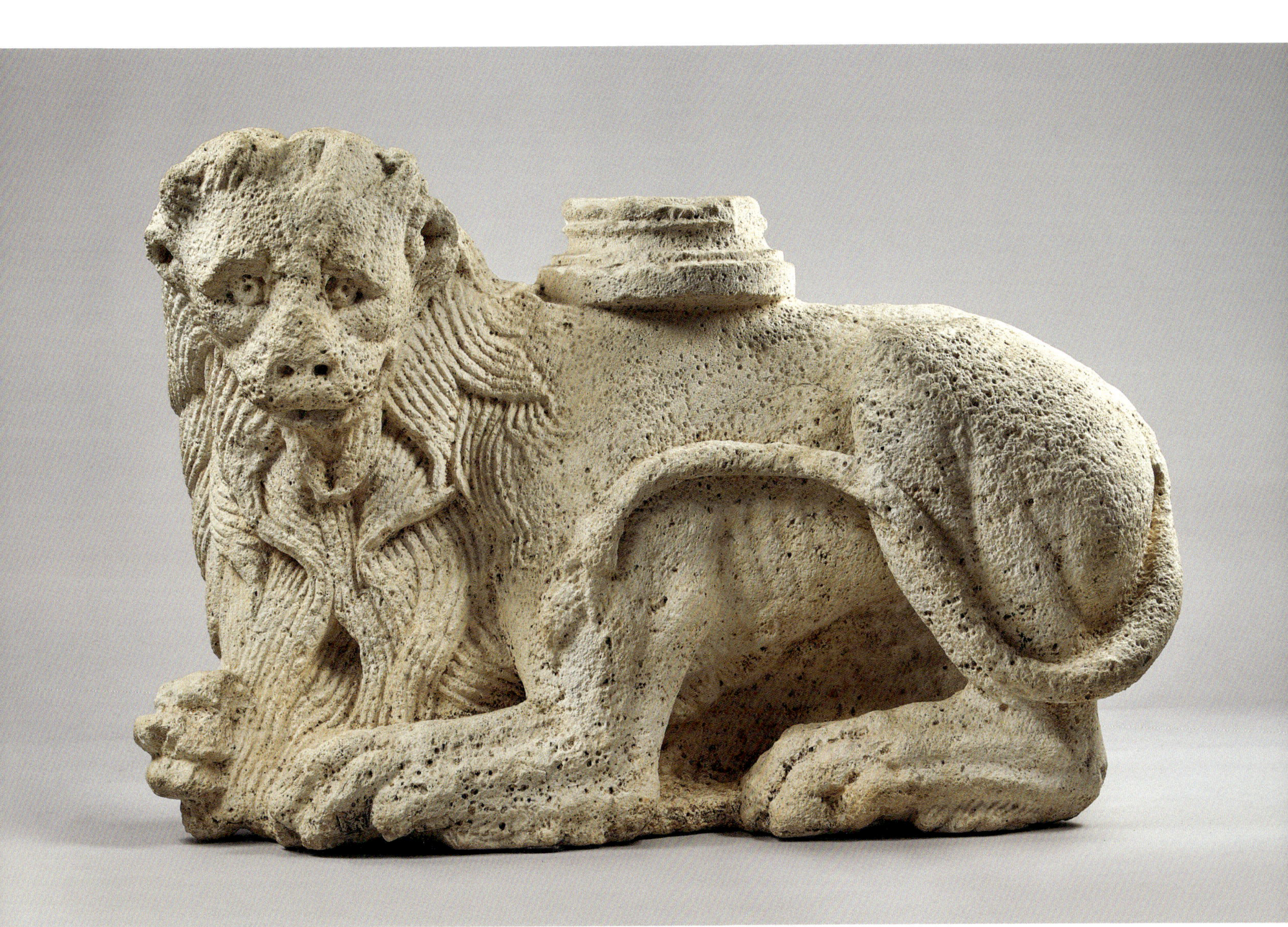

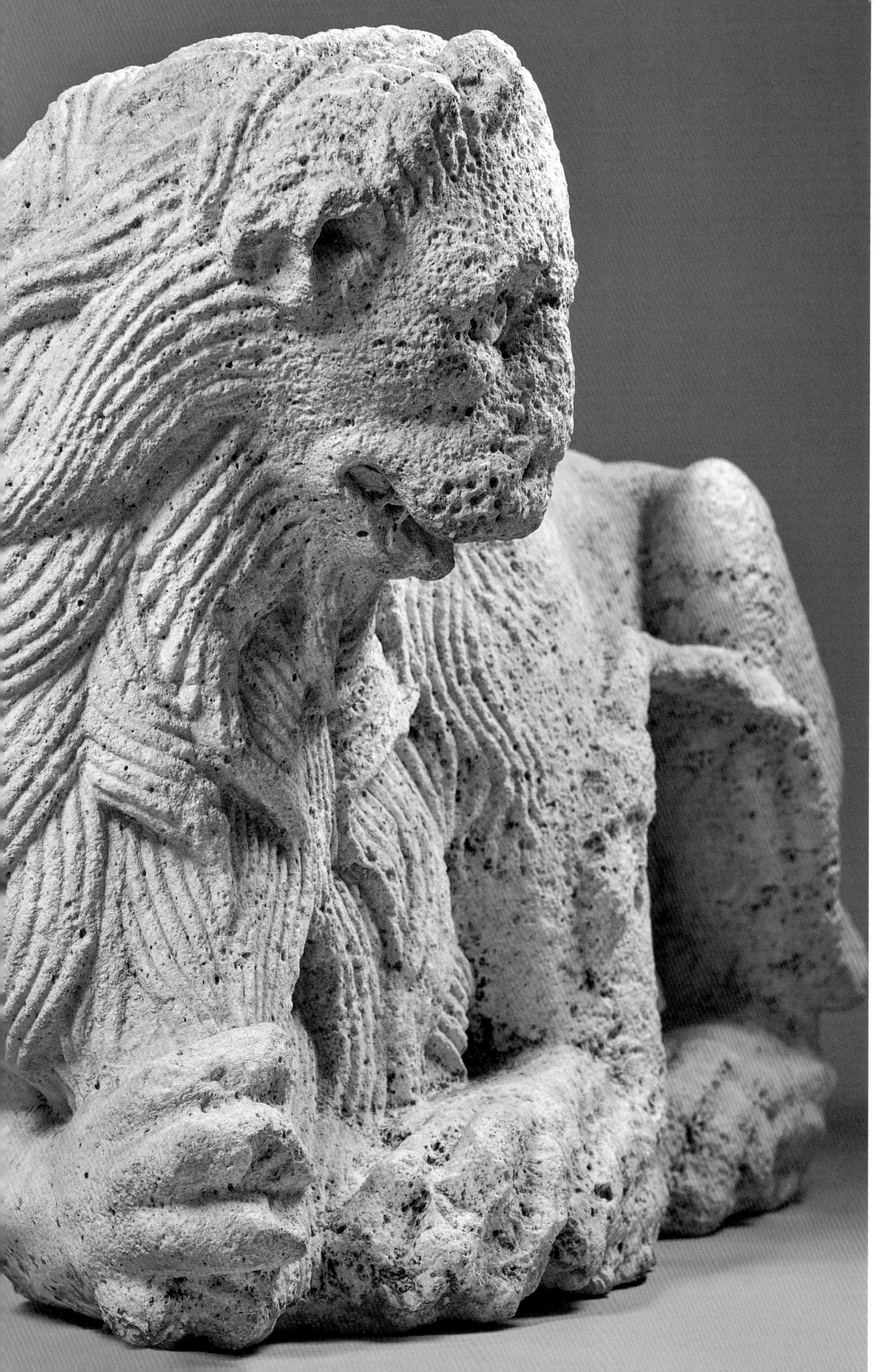

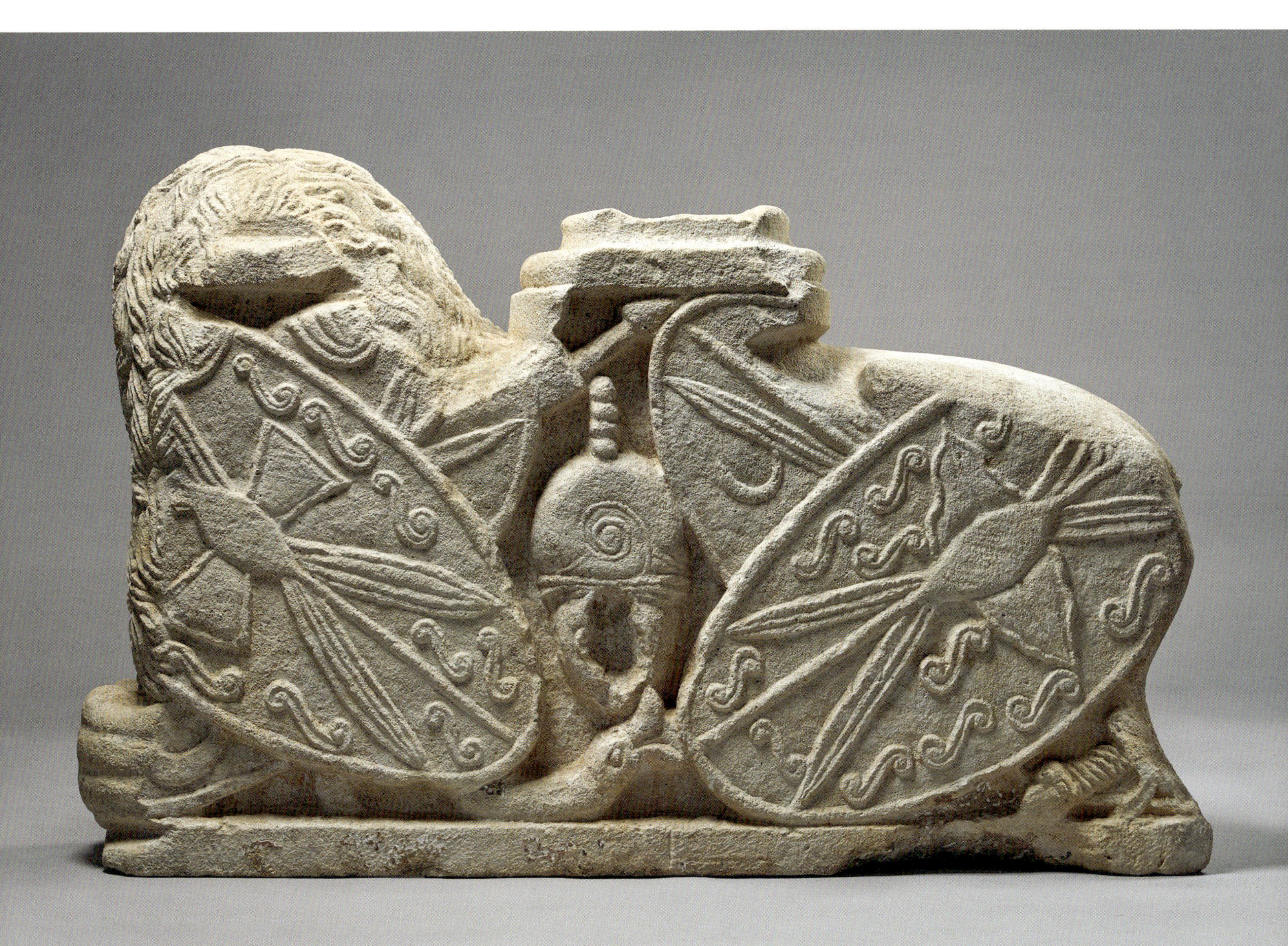

8 **Manuscript leaf with two scenes: a couple discussing legalities with lawyers, and two lovers in a bed**
Southern France, Toulouse (?)
*c.*1320
42.5 × 29 cm / 16.7 × 11.4 in.
Ink, pigments and gilding on parchment, from a copy of
Gratian's Decretals

PROVENANCE
Private collection, Germany; McCarthy collection, London,
since 2006

PUBLISHED
Kidd (2021), 235–243.

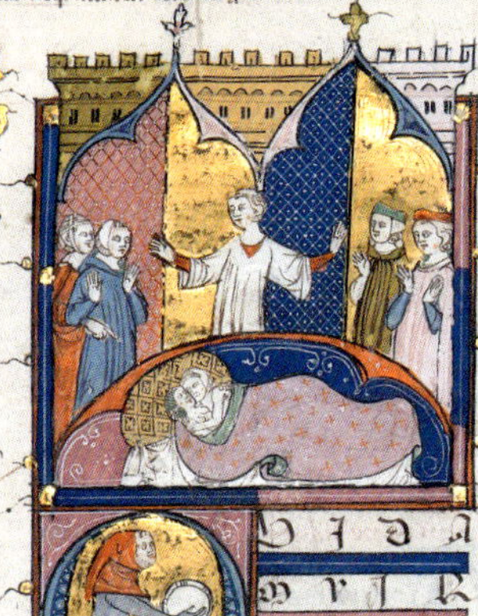

s aut mulier qo non possit sibi redde debitum ppt naturalem fri
dicatem. Jo.
tunest in primo libro capitulari karoli. s. in lombarda. Jo.
ne. ar qo quandoqp mulieri defertur pbo anno coniuncte carius

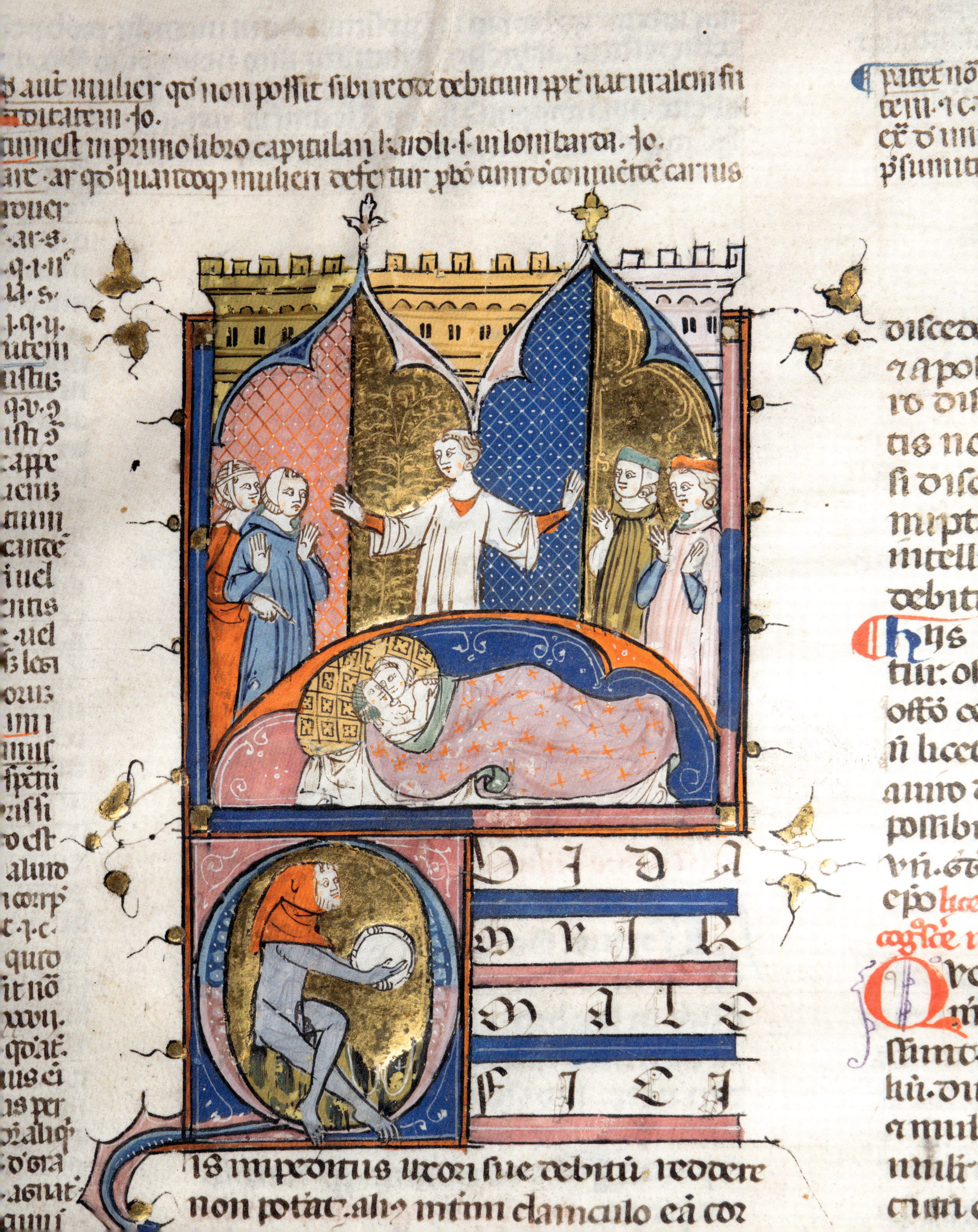

is impeditus uxori sue debitu redde
non potuat. Aliqui infm clamauilo ea cor

9 **Aquamanile in the form of a lion**
Germany, Nuremberg
*c.*1350
27 × 25.5 × 11 cm / 10.5 × 10 × 4.3 in.
Hollow cast copper alloy

PROVENANCE
Private European collection (purchased
in Burgundy, 1990s)

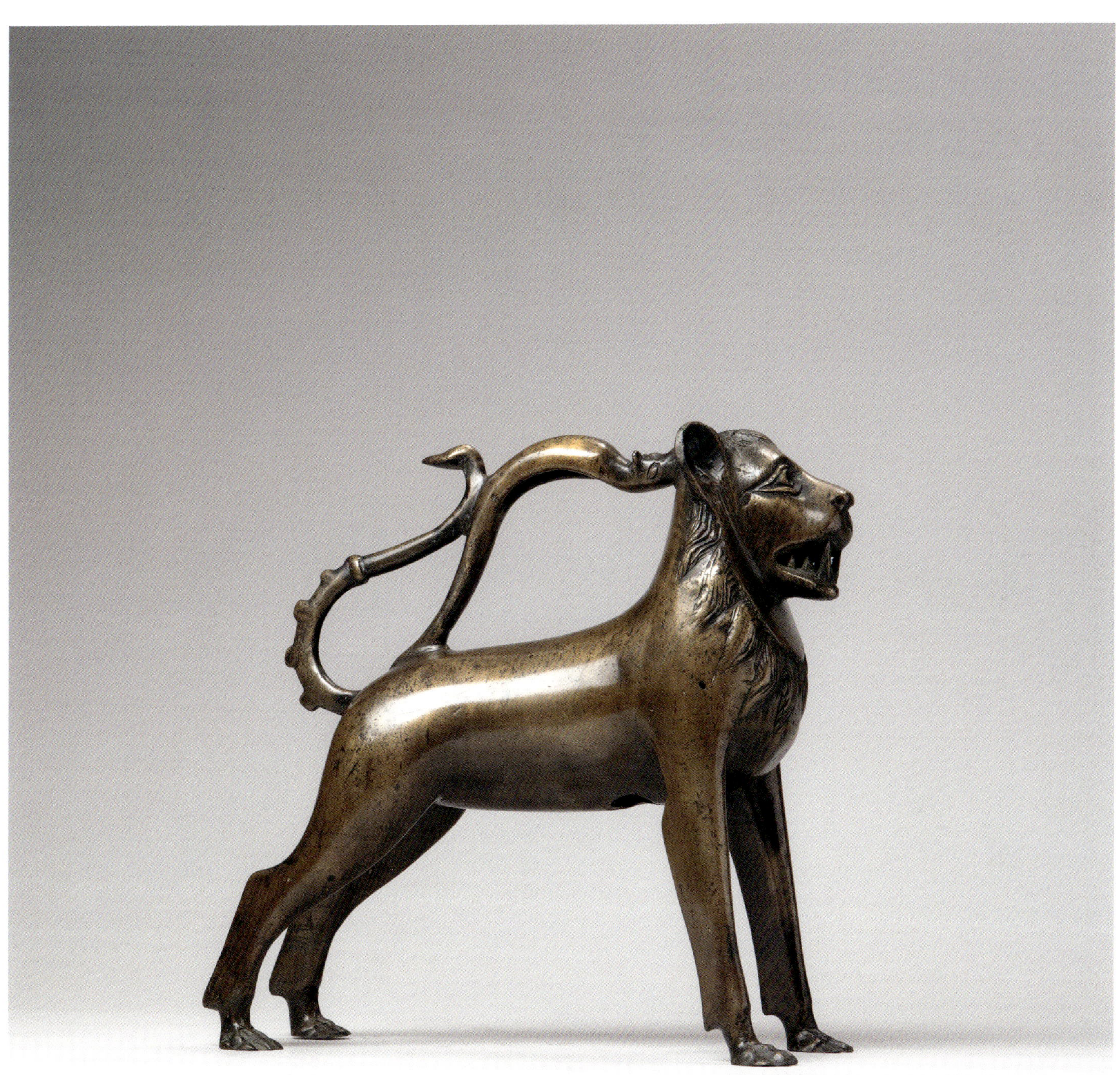

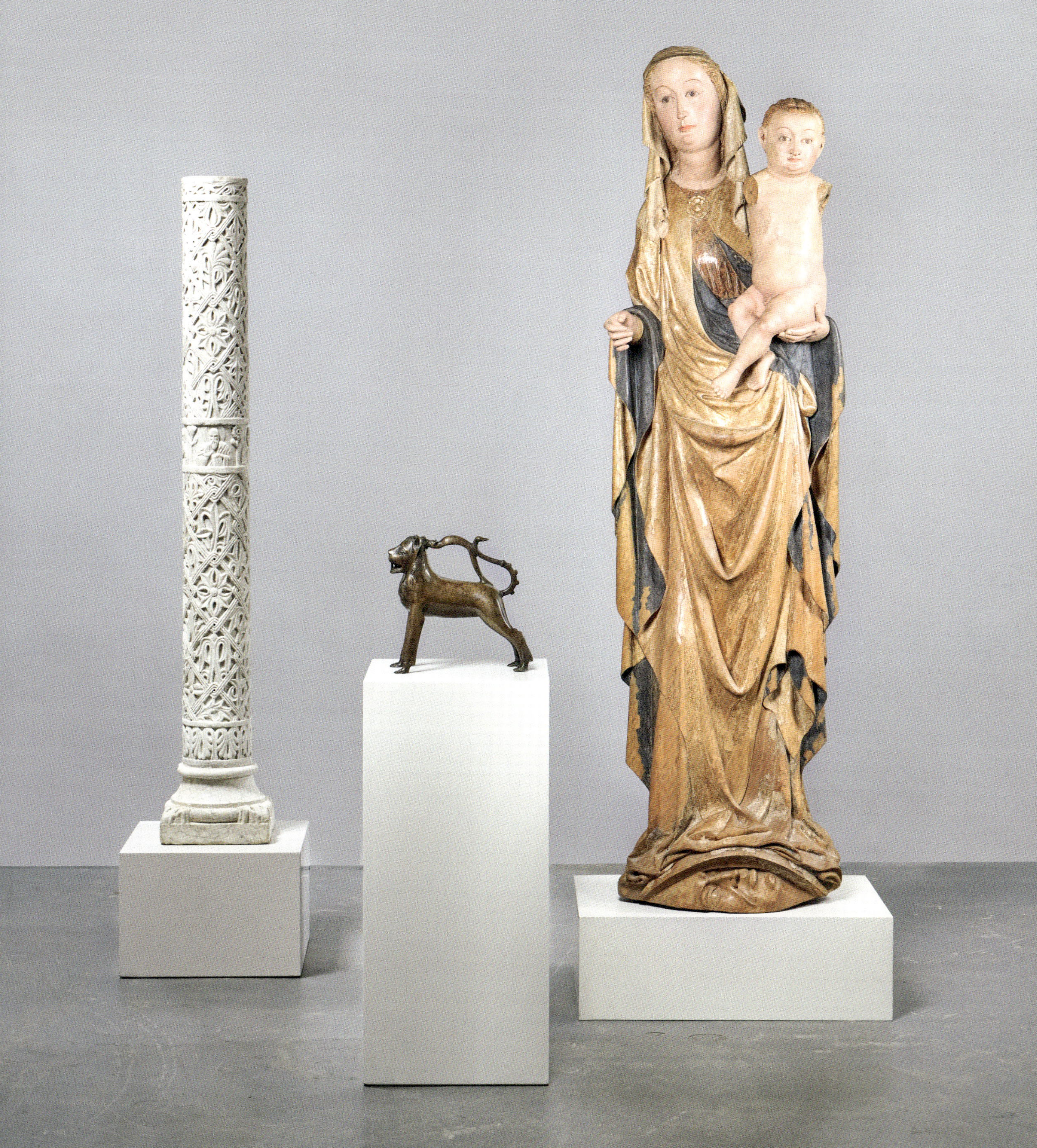

10

The Chaworth Roll
A genealogy of the kings of England tracing the royal succession from Ebgert to Henry IV, with a map of roads of England and a Wheel of Fortune
England, in Anglo-Norman and French
1321–1327, with additions between 1399 and 1413
642 × 24.5 cm / 252.7 × 9.6 in.
Ink and pigments on nine joined sheets of lined parchment

PROVENANCE
Believed to have been commissioned by Thomas Chaworth of Wiverton (1290–1347), *c.*1320s; By decent in the Chaworth Musters family until 1988; Robert Holden Ltd, London, 1988; Martin Schoyen collection, Norway, MS 250; Deaccessioned in 2013; McCarthy collection, London.

PUBLISHED
Godwin (1883–85), 197–9; Beal and Griffiths (1992), 272–273, 279–280, 282, 284; Griffiths (1995), 36–42, MS 250; de Laborderie (1997), 185–193; Bovey (2005); de Laborderie (2014); Kidd (2019) 76–81.

EXHIBITED
Presented by E. W. Godwin to the Society of Antiquaries, London (1885); Conference of European National Librarians, Oslo, September 1994; *European medieval manuscripts from The Schøyen Collection*, University of Oslo. Domus Bibliotheca, 6–15 May 1996

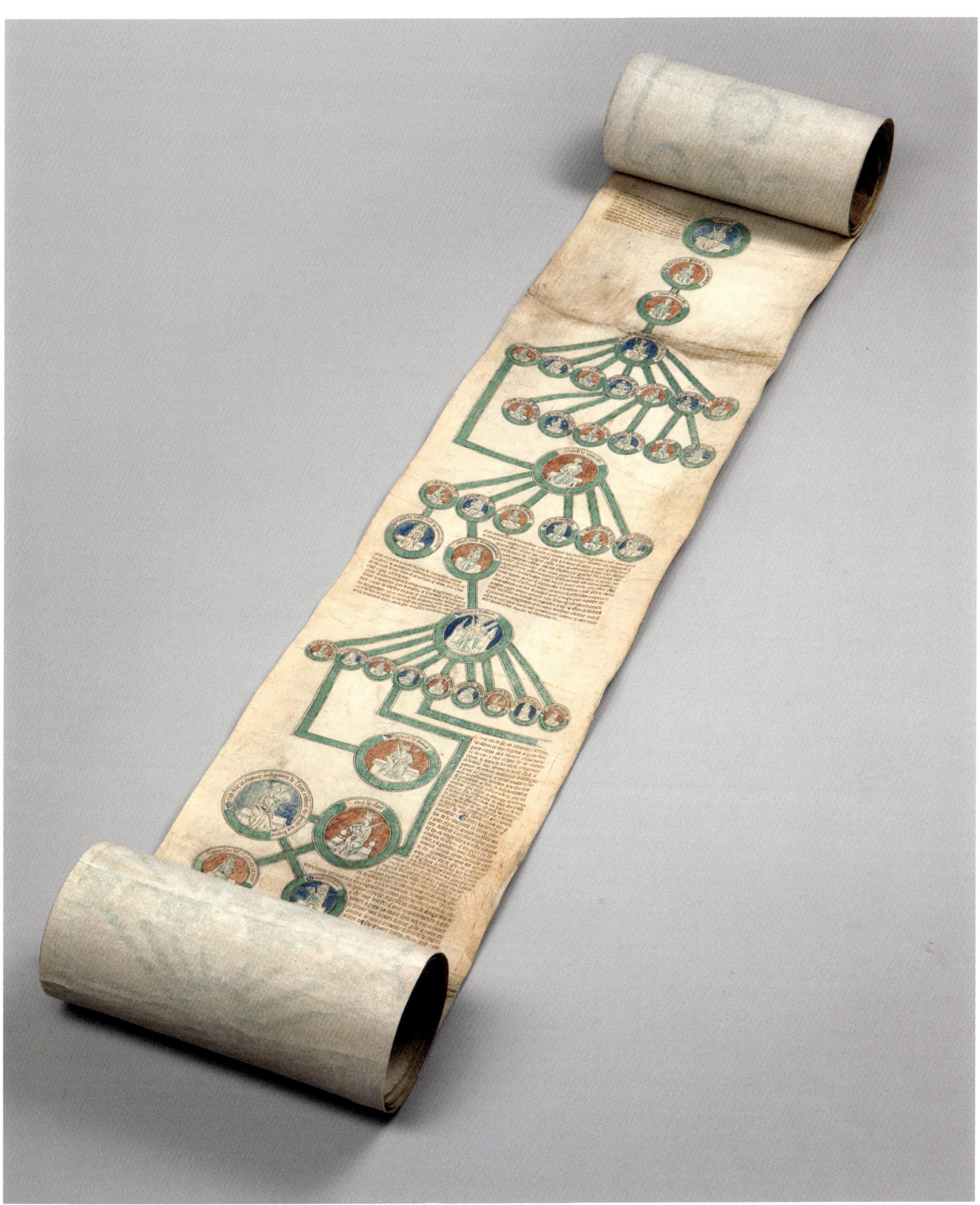

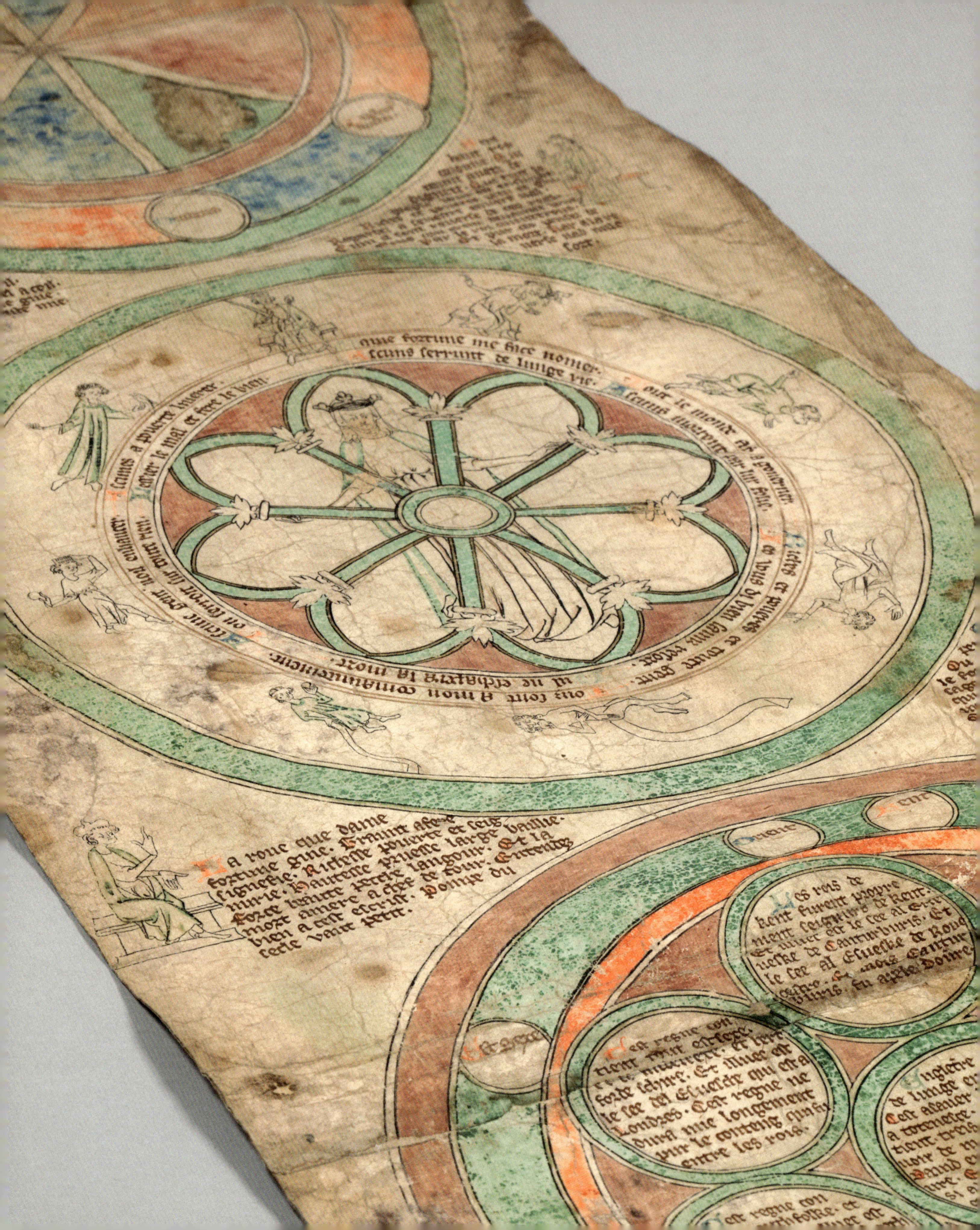

Quue fortune me fice nomer.
scuns serunt de luigr vie.
La roue que dame
fortune fine. Pruint aseȝ
signefie. Richece puuent et seig
nurie. Hautece puuent larȝe ve
fort uuire ferre langouur. de uuir
mort amere a ceo de fortune
bien a cest escrit. pour du
cest uuit xxxii.

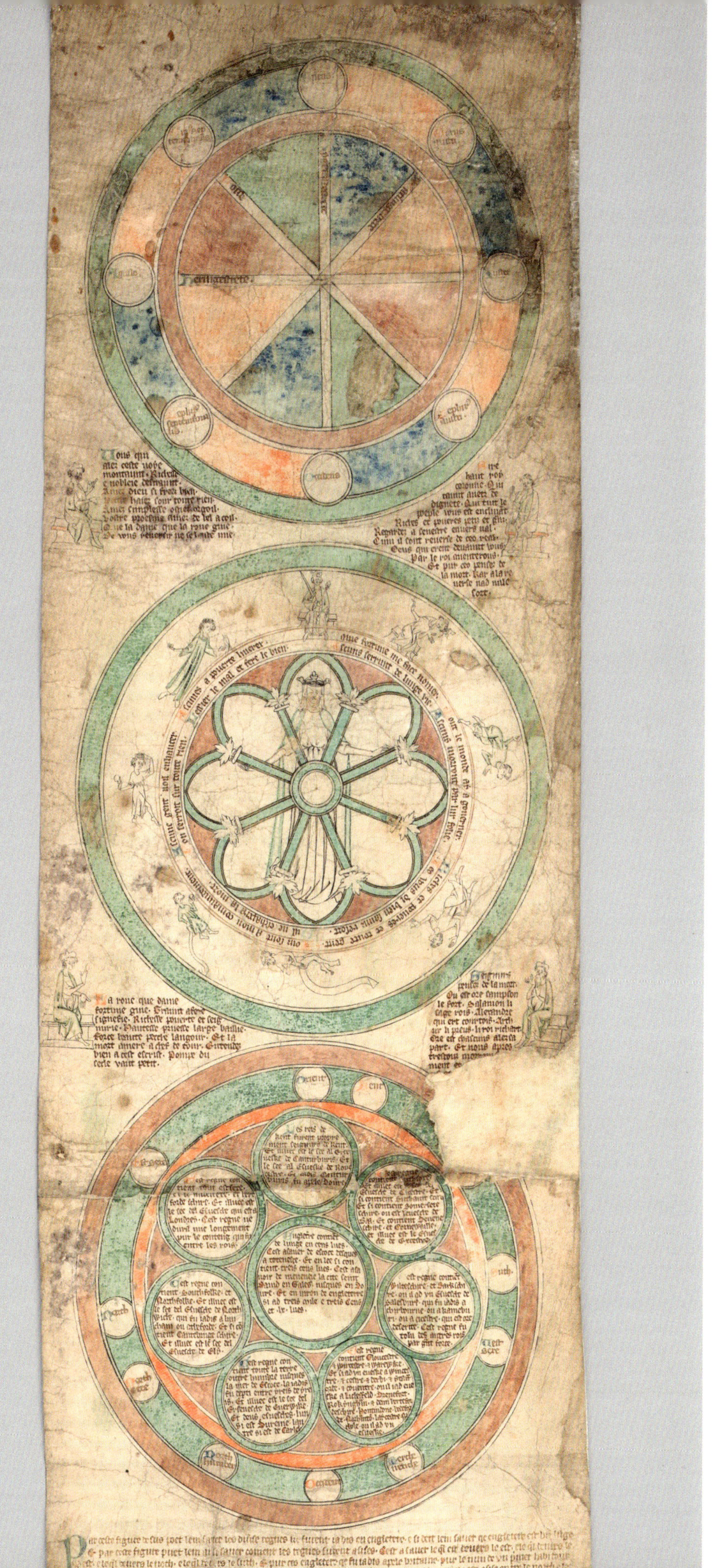

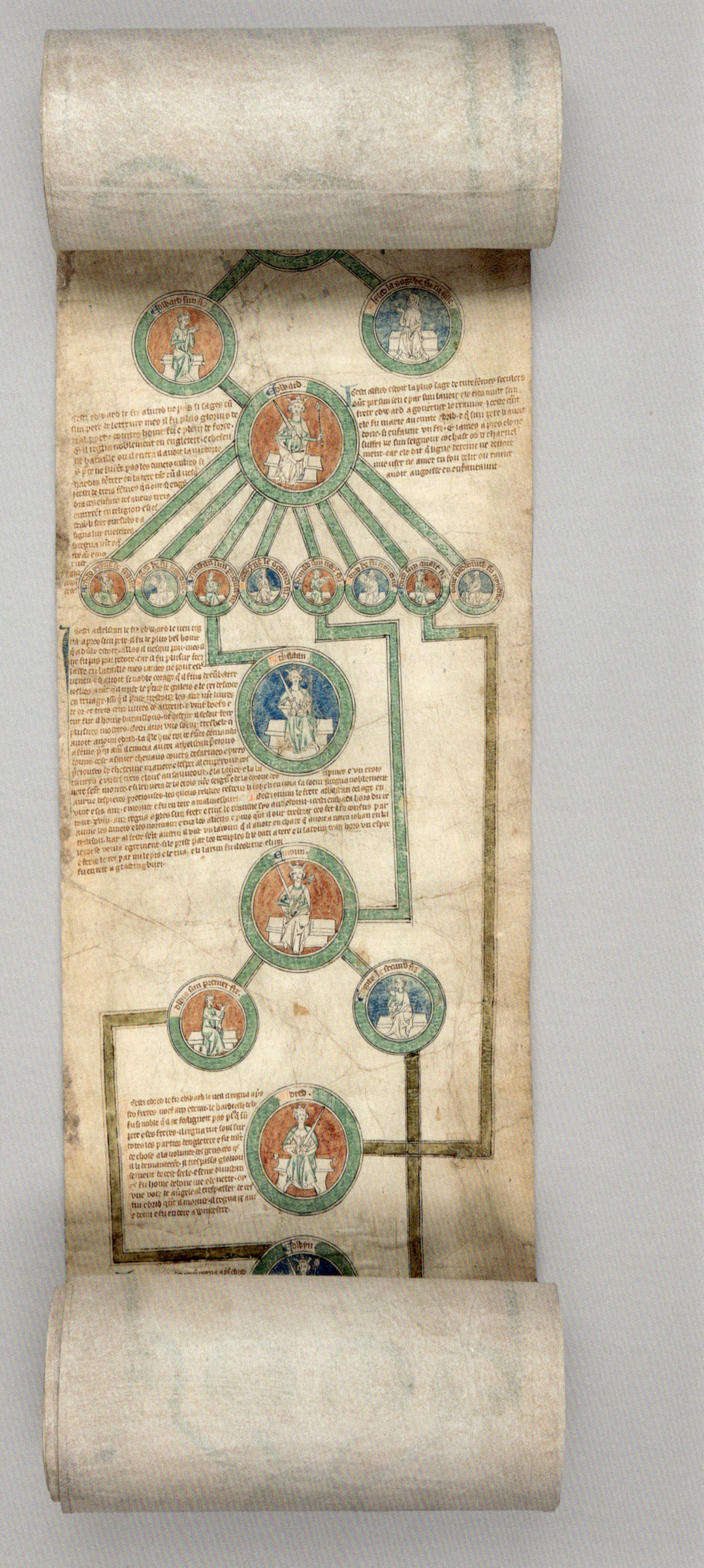

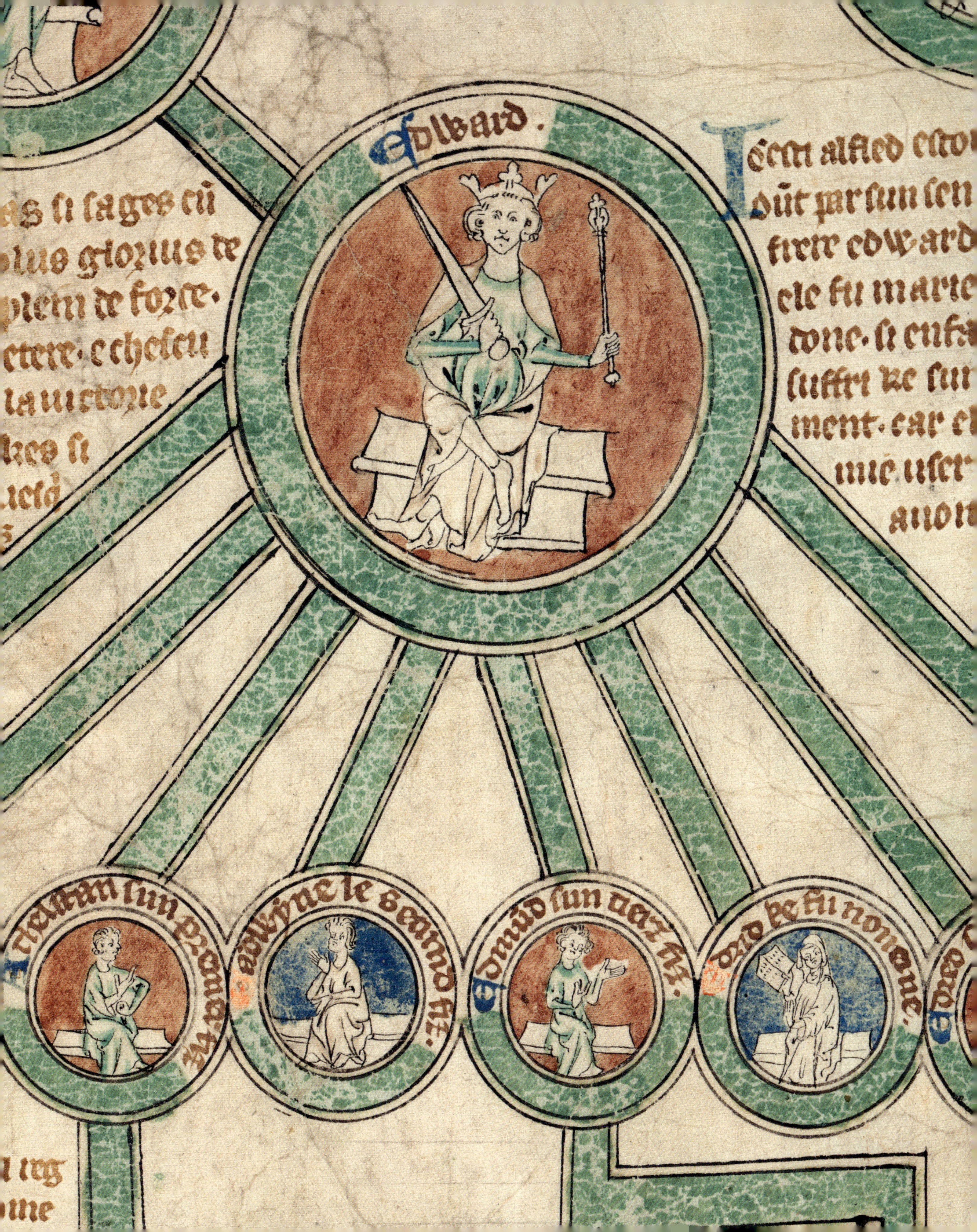
Edward.
Aelstan sun p(re)mer fiz
Edwyne le secund fiz
Edmund sun tierz fiz
...ed le fiz nome...
...es li sages cu(m)...
...lus glorius te...
...plein de force...
...terre · e chesu...
...la victorie...
...kes si...
...ield...
com alfred esto...
dut par sun sen...
frere edward...
ele fu mariee...
done · si enfa(n)...
suffri ke su(n)...
ment · car e...
nue uset...
anon...

11 **The Berkeley Purse**
Opus Anglicanum
The Crucifixion and The Coronation of the Virgin
England
c.1320–1330
25.1 × 25.9 cm / 10 × 10.1 in. (Coronation), 24.7 × 26
cm / 9.7 × 10.2 in. (Crucifixion); Embroidery of silver-
gilt thread and coloured silks on linen

PROVENANCE
Robert Valentine Berkeley (1853–1940); The Berkeley
Collection, Spetchley Park, by 1905; and by descent
until 2019.

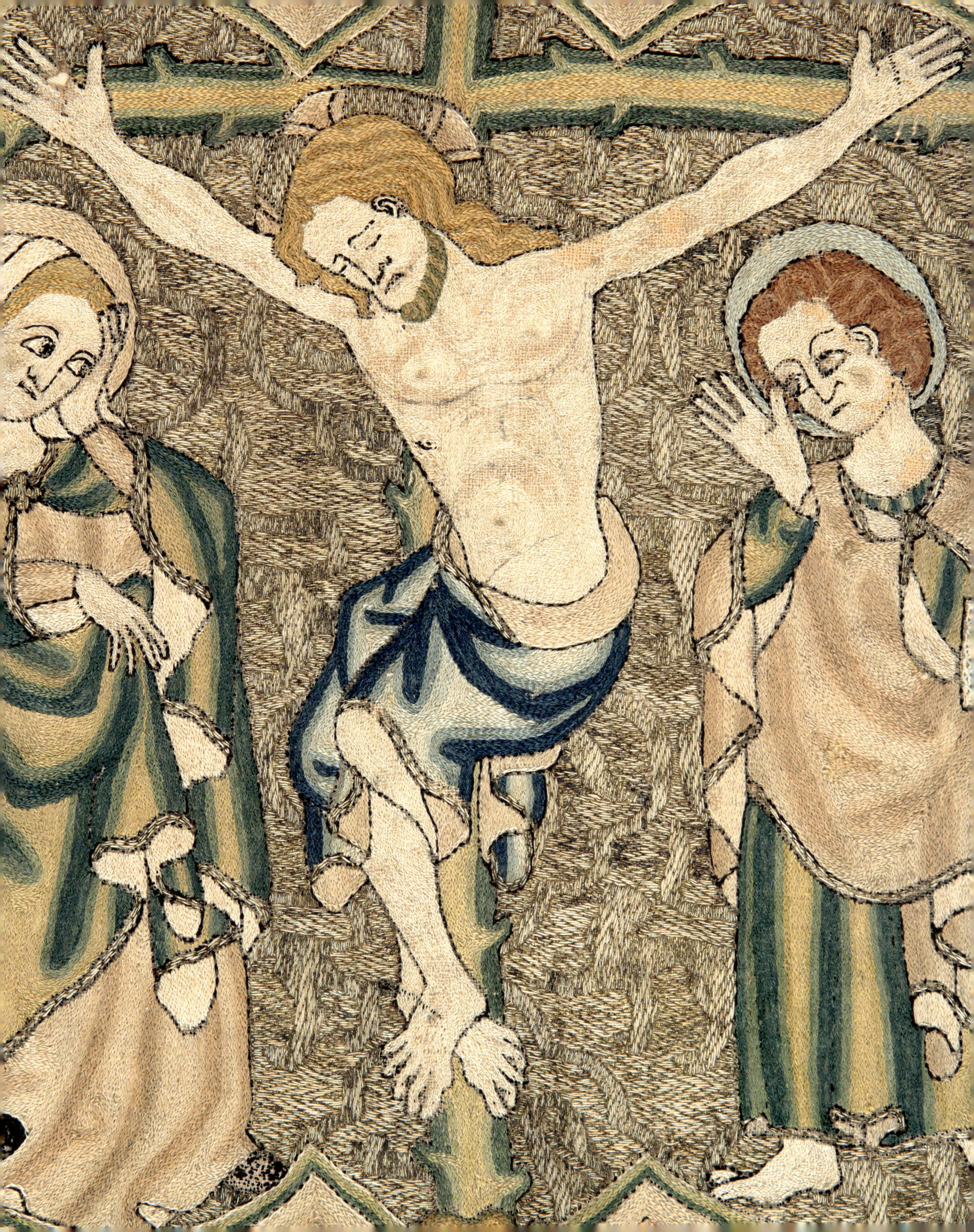

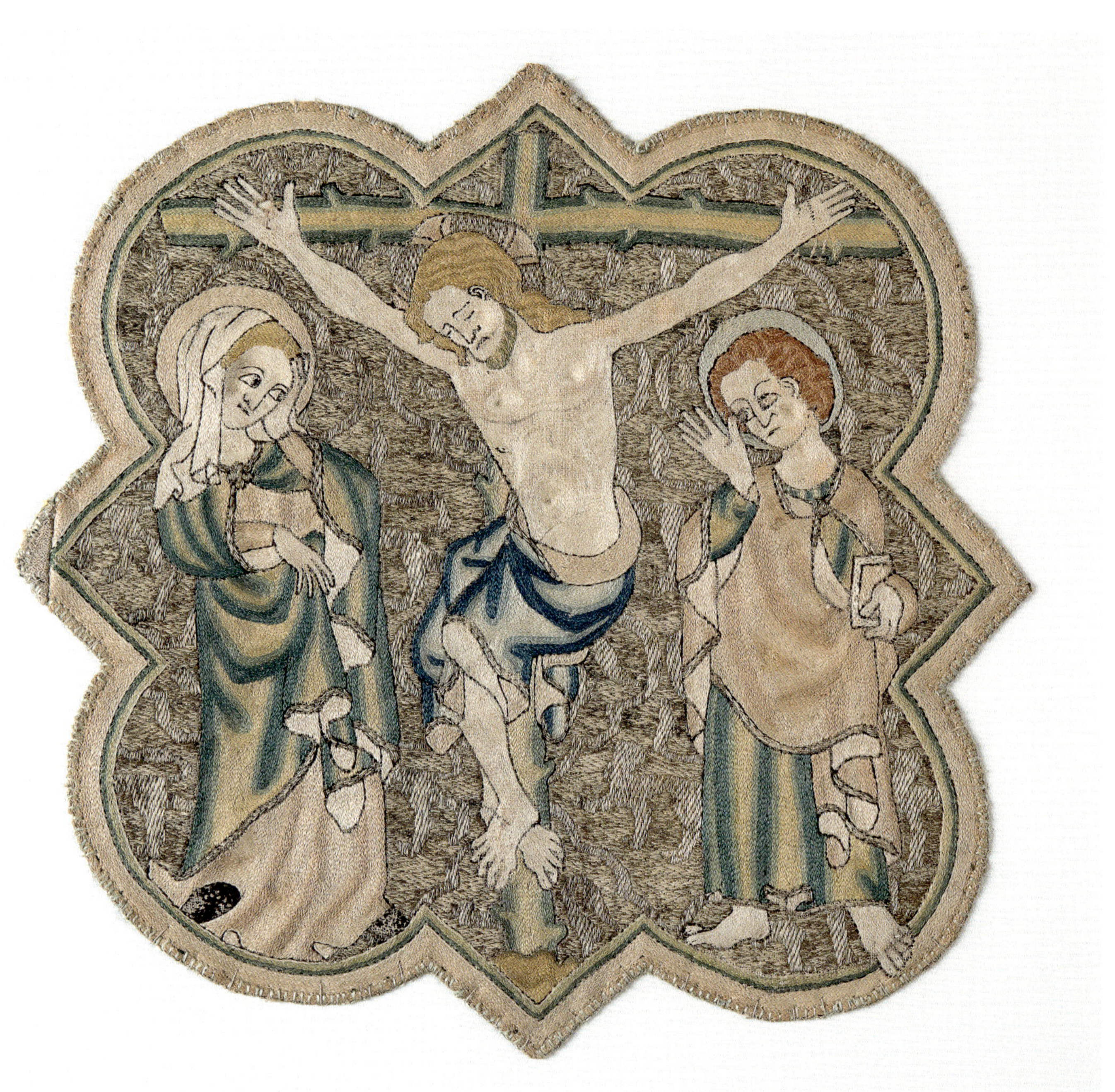

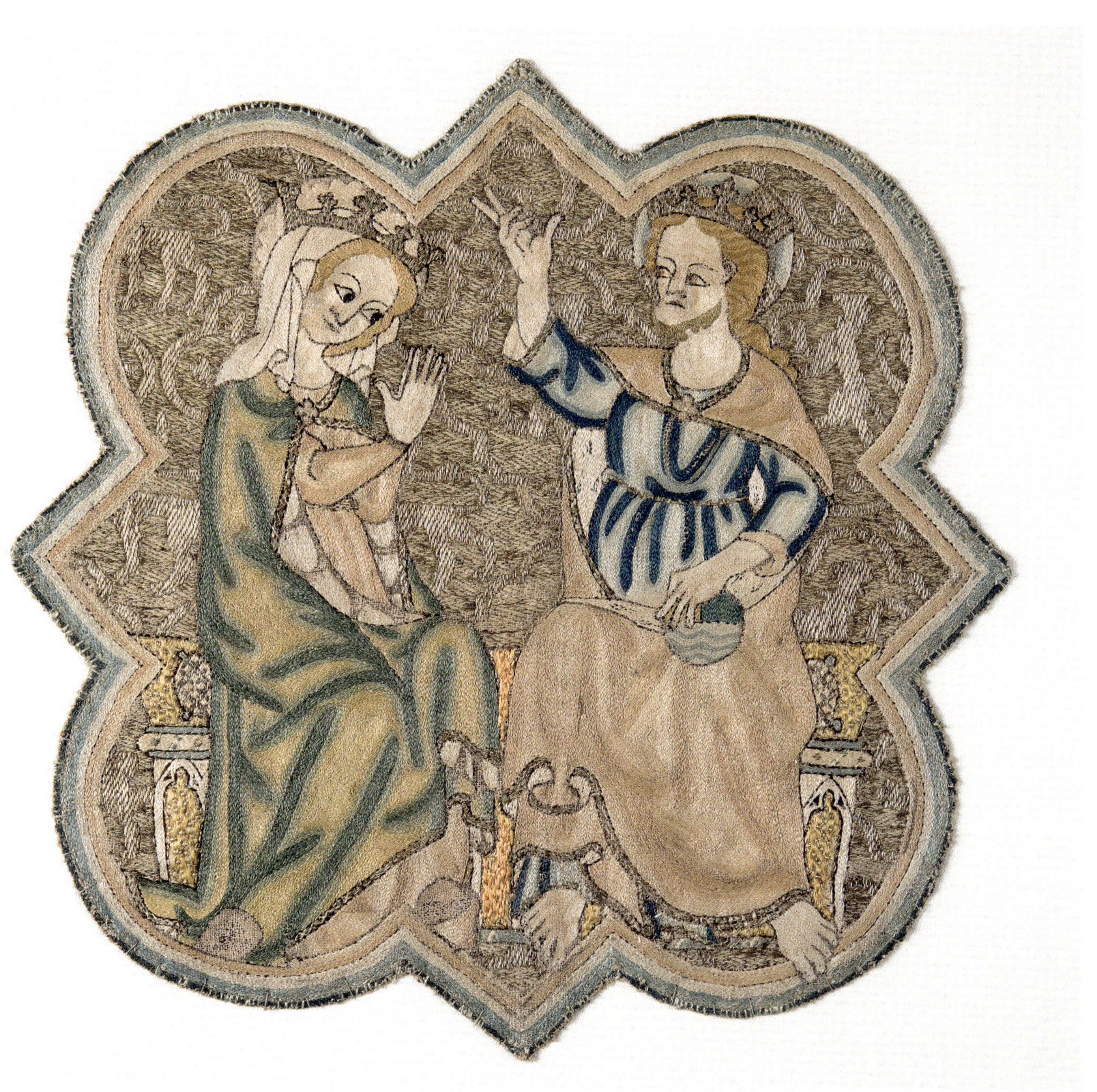

12

**A Monumental 'Beautiful Madonna'
(Schöne Madonna)**
Kingdom of Bohemia
*c.*1420–1440
175 × 50 × 24 cm / 68.9 × 19.7 × 9.4 in.
Polychromy and gilding on poplar

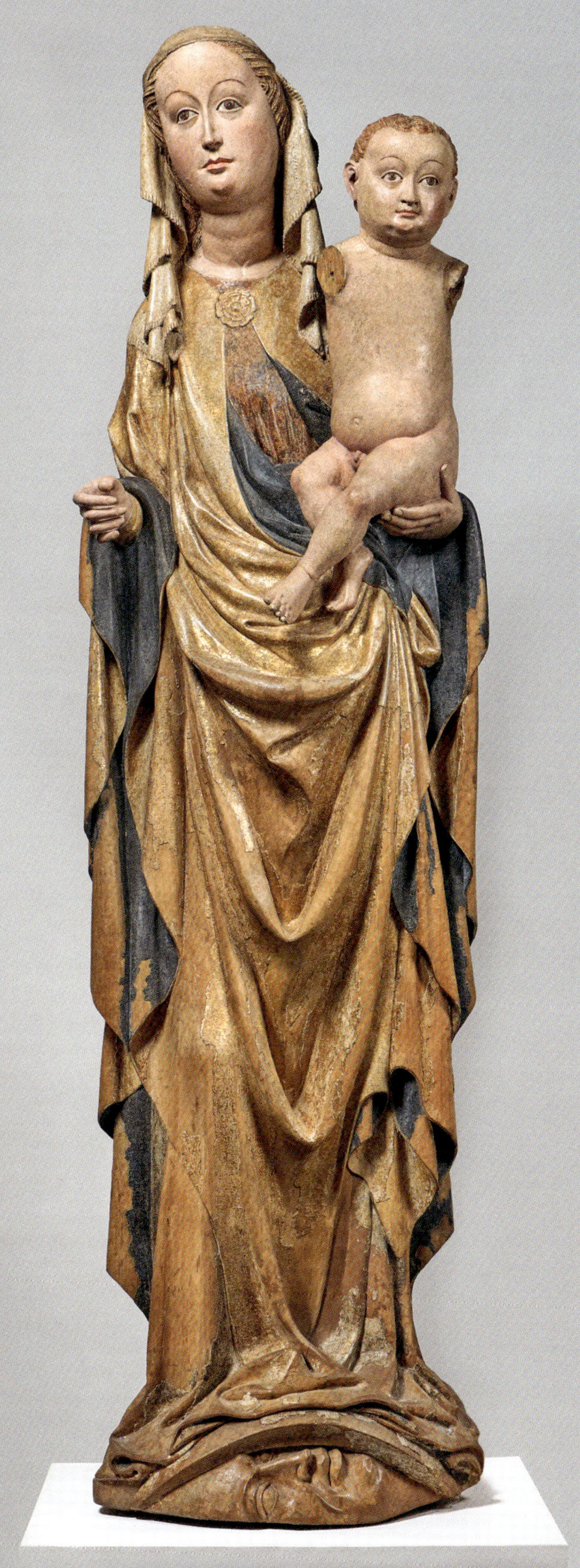

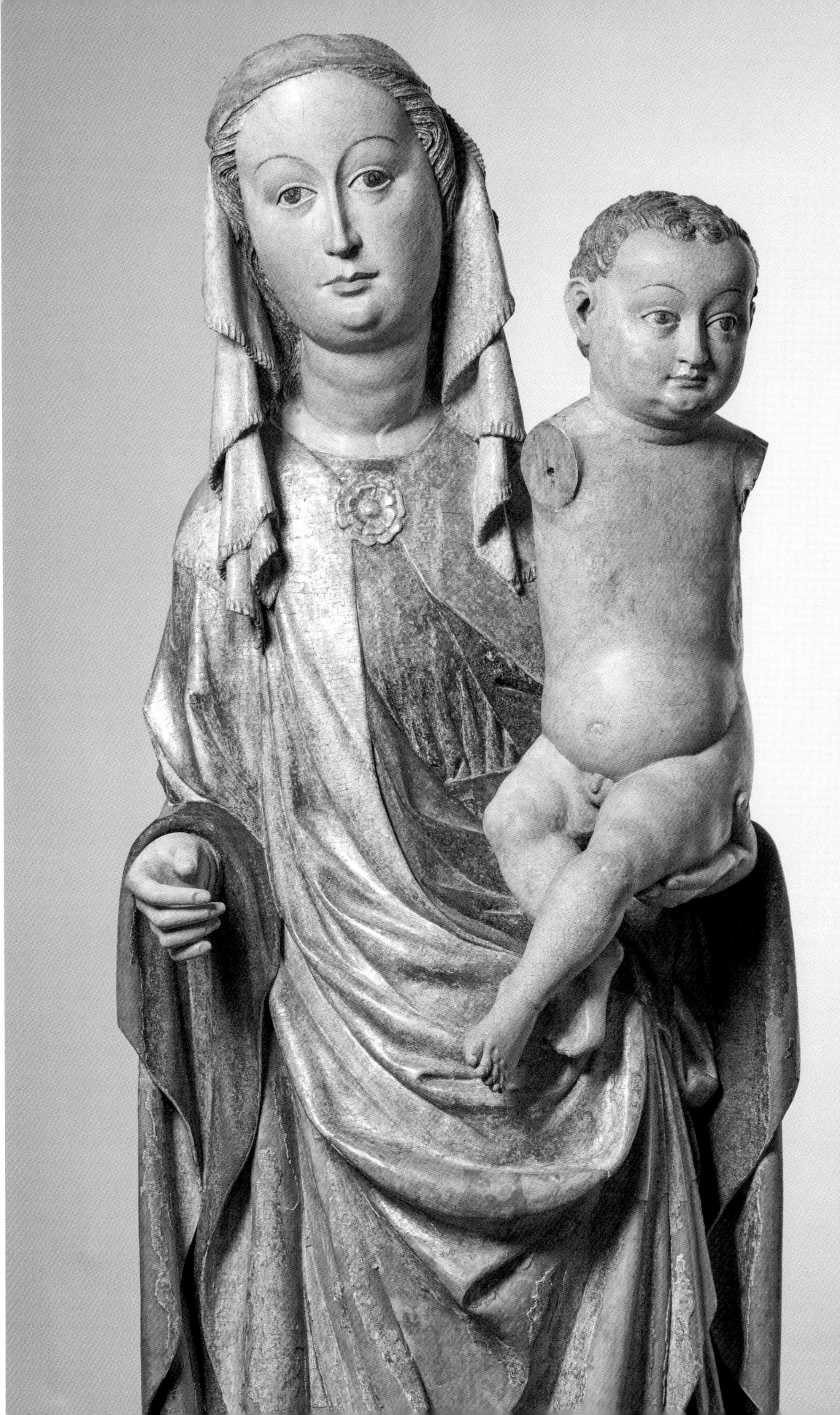

13

Saint Quentin being tormented
France, Picardy, Amiens (?)
*c.*1420–1430
100 × 87 × 22 cm / 39.4 × 34.3 × 8.7 in.
Limestone with traces of early polychromy

PROVENANCE
Jacqueline Boccador, Paris, by 1974

PUBLISHED
Boccador (1974), 48 and front cover.

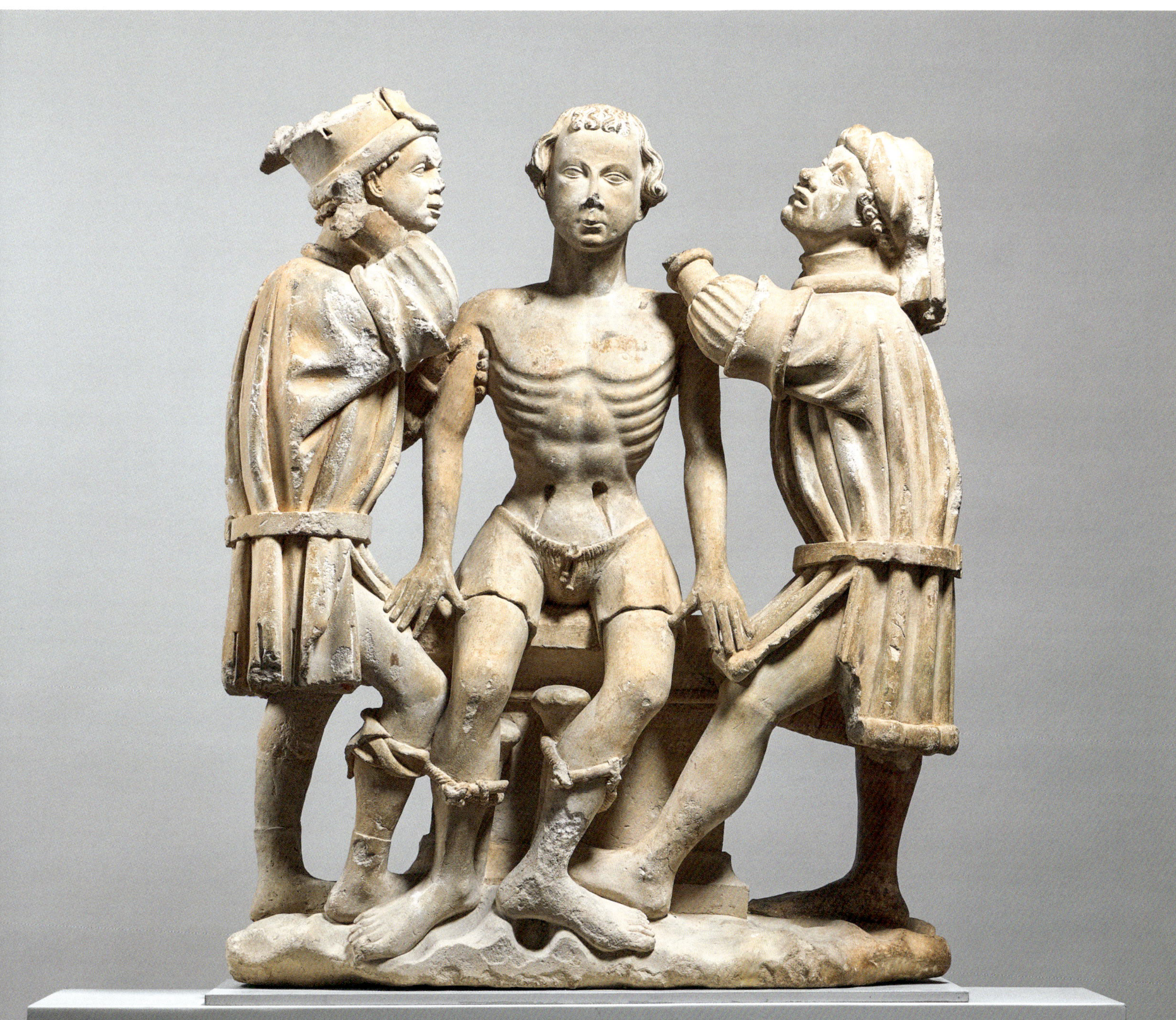

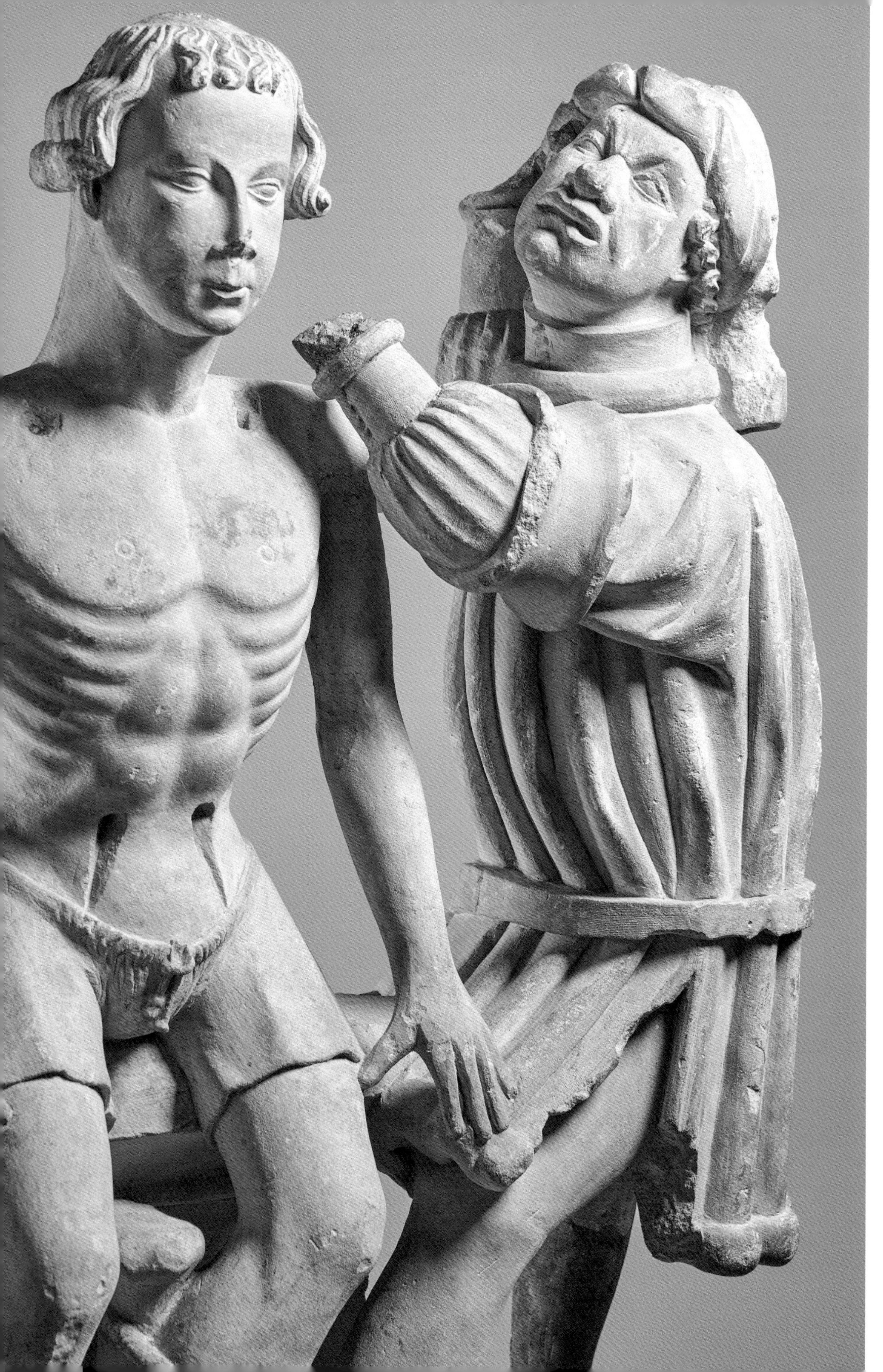

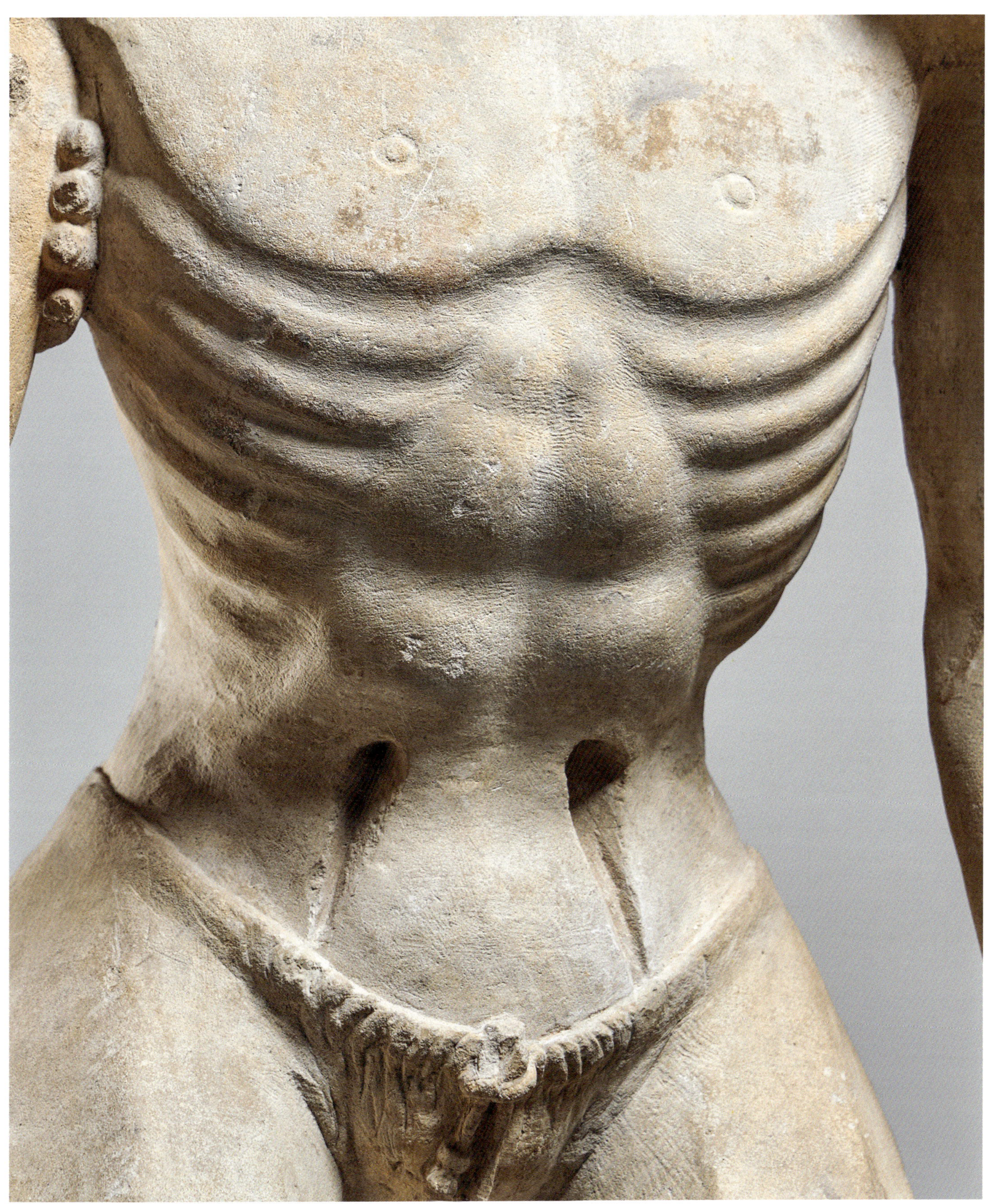

14 **THE MASTER OF THE HOLY KINSHIP** (active 1410–1440)
The Man of Sorrows accompanied by a kneeling Donor

Germany, Cologne
*c.*1410–1440
120 × 64 cm / 47.2 × 25.2 in.
Oil and gilding on panel

PROVENANCE

Heinz Kisters Collection, Kreutzlingen; thence by descent until 2018.

PUBLISHED

Stange (1967), No. 44 (as Veronica Master); Theuerkauff-Liederwald
(1988), 126, figure 13; Chapuis (2004), 217; Pieper (1970) (as Veronika
Master); Zehnder (1990), 327, (as Master of the Holy Kinship);
Zehnder, (1993), 308, No. 39 (as Master of the Holy Kinship).

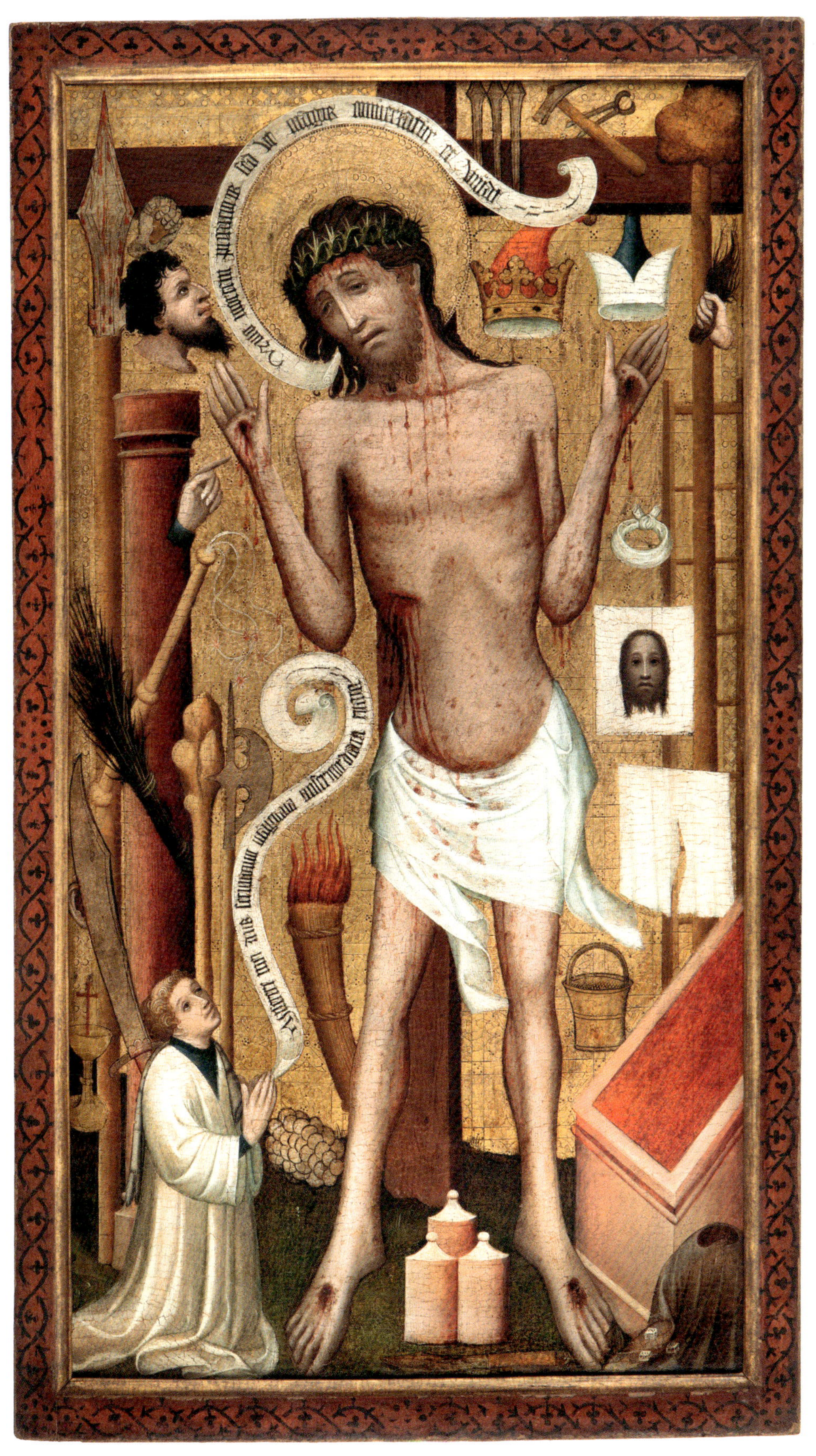

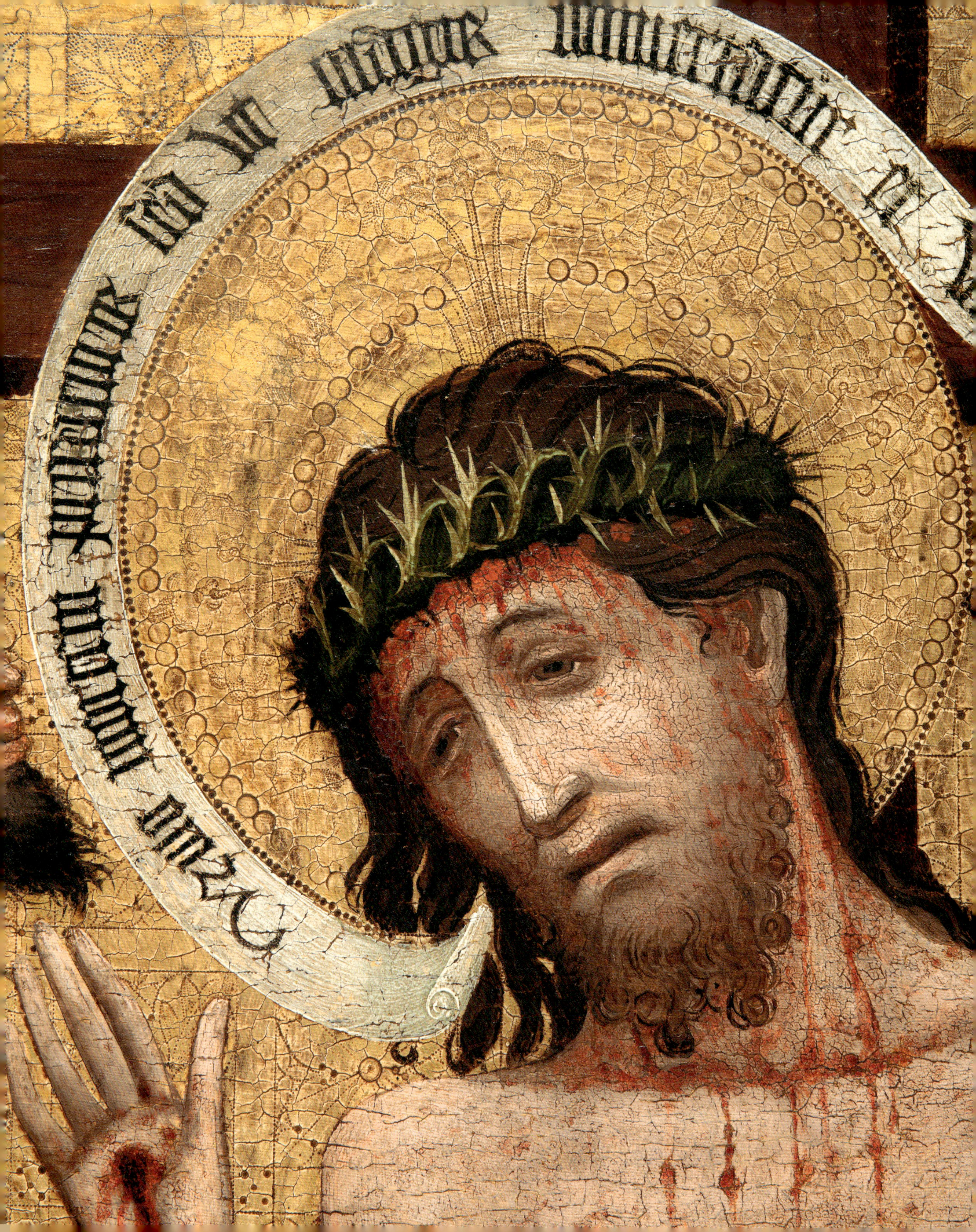

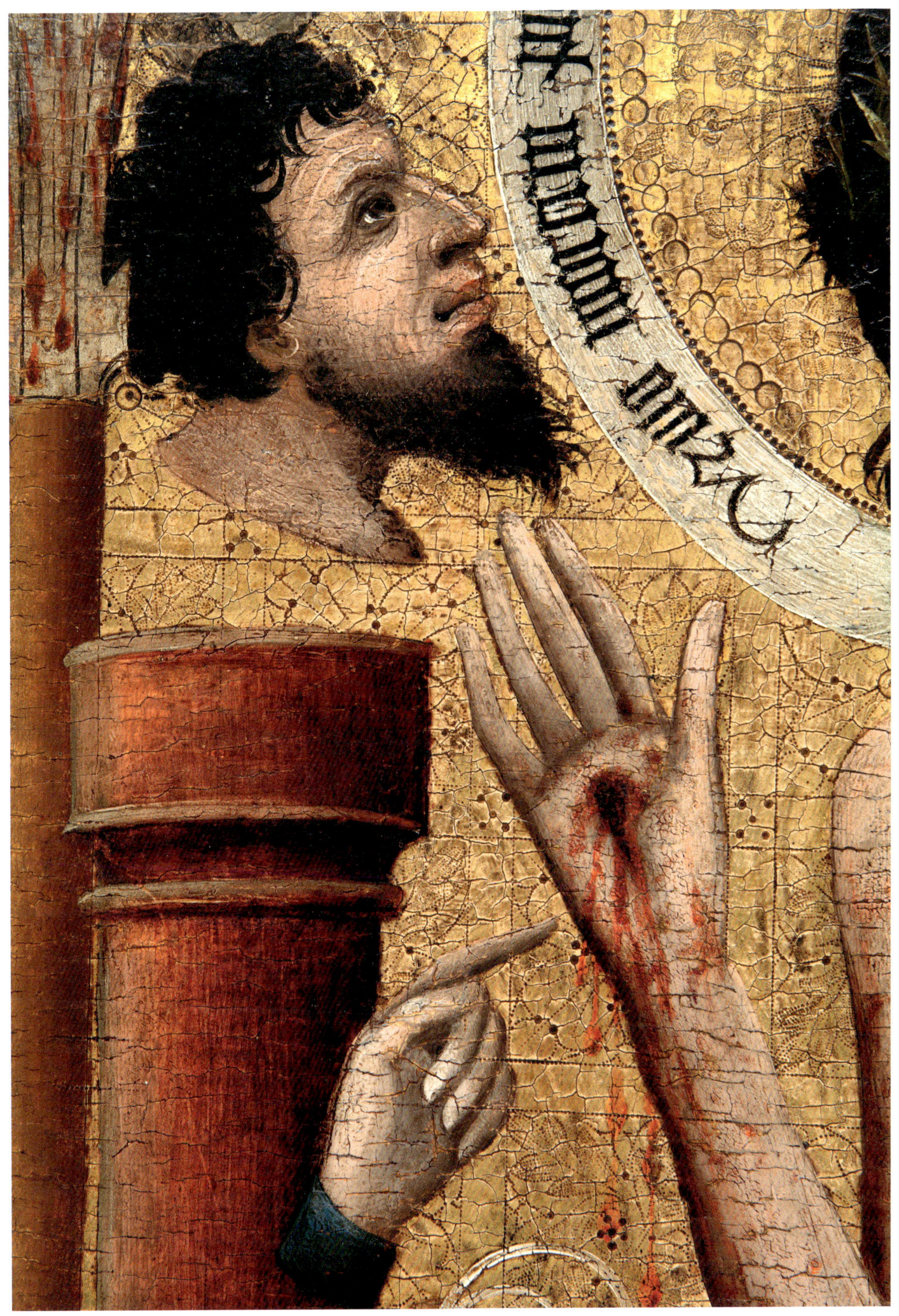

15

A pair of alabaster standing Apostles, carved for the high altar of Saint-Omer Cathedral
Southern Netherlands or Northern France
*c.*1430 (probably 1429)
23.7 × 9.3 × 5.8 cm / 9.3 × 3.7 × 2.3 in. (bearded Apostle);
23.7 × 10.2 × 5.9 cm / 9.3 × 4 × 2.32 in. (Saint John);
alabaster with the original gilding largely intact

PROVENANCE
Collection of Augustin Ozenfant (1834–1894), Lille, acquired 1864; Thence by descent to Chanoine Paul Bernard, Lille, until 1962; Dr. Albert Habart, Calais, until 1971; Julius Böhler, Munich; Collection of David and Louise Carter, New Haven, acquired from the above in 1973.

EXHIBITED
Exposition d'objets d'art religieux, Lille, l'Hôtel de l'ancienne Préfecture du Nord, 14 June–13 July 1874, nos. 554 and 555

PUBLISHED
Drivel (1876), 135, nos. 554 and 555; *Rhein und Maas*, (1972); Steyaert (1994), 327.

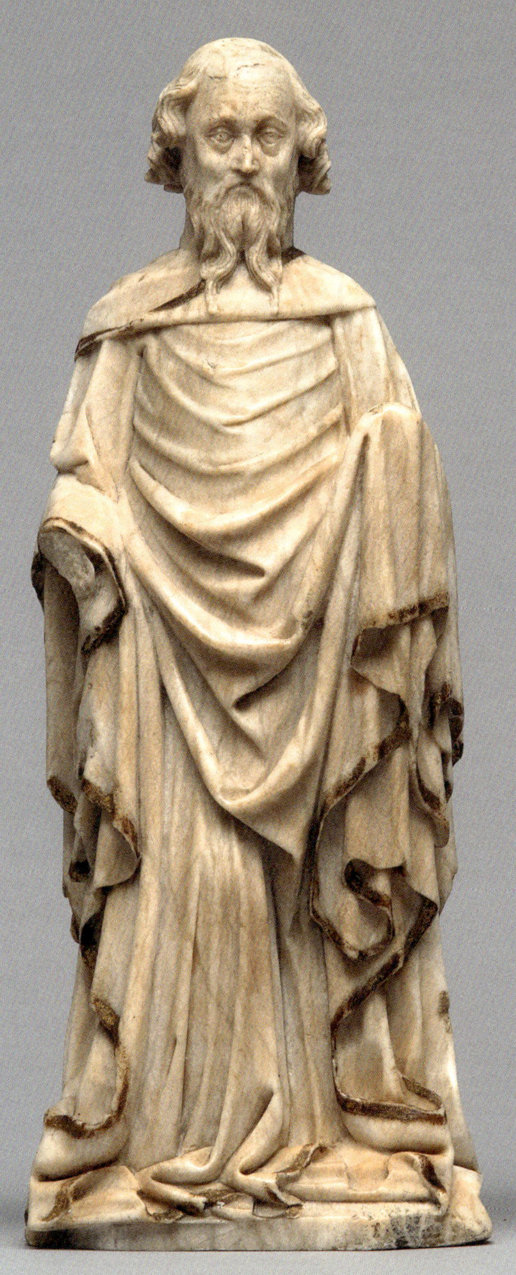
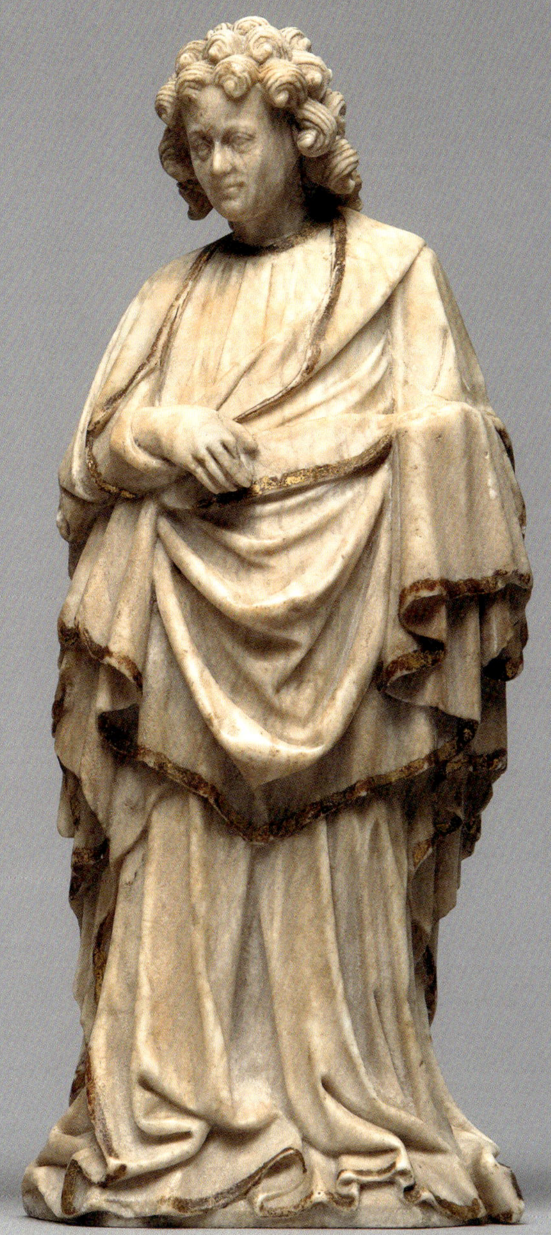

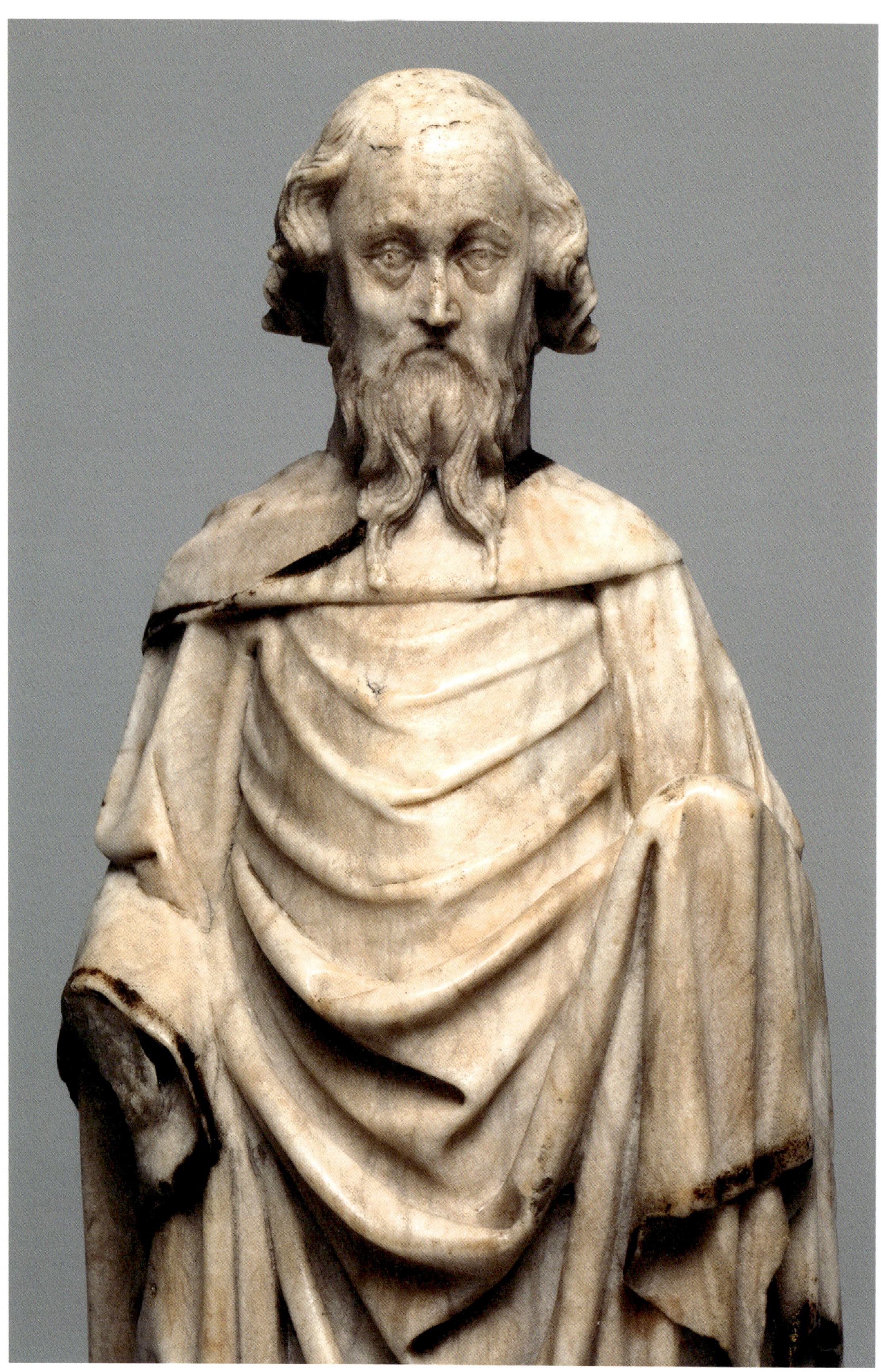

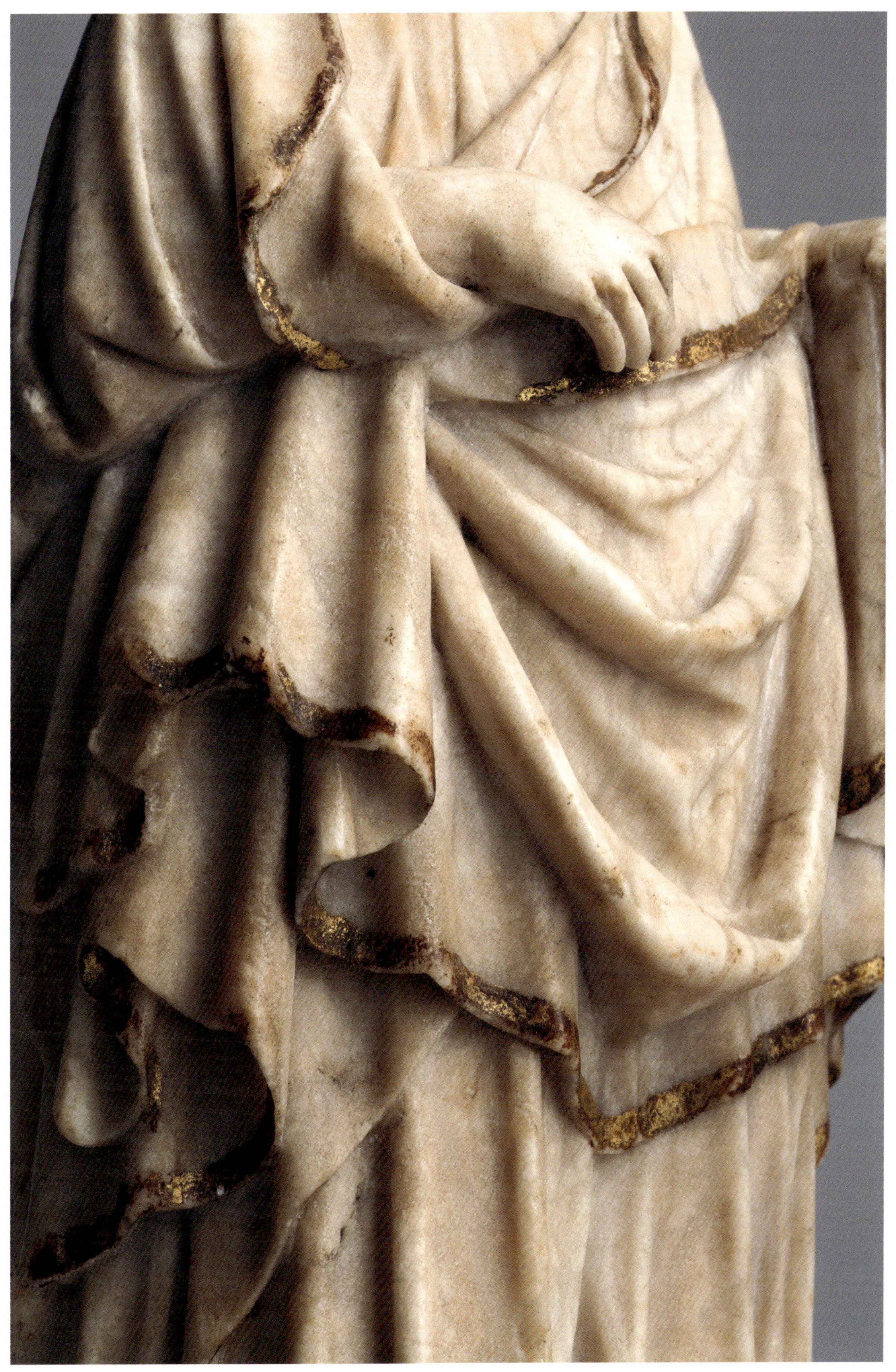

16   A micro-architectural custodia for the display of relics

Northern Spain

*c.*1450, with feet attended by small fighting men added from a late
fifteenth-century structure

44.7 × 22.8 × 17.6 cm / 17.6 × 9 × 6.9 in.

Gilded silver with cast, hammered, chased and engraved elements
with panels enamelled in green and blue glass

PROVENANCE

Collection of Baron James de Rothschild (1878–1957); His
posthumous sale, 'Collection du Baron James de Rothschild',
Palais Galliéra, 1st December 1966, lot 221; Private collection,
Austria, and by descent until 2020.

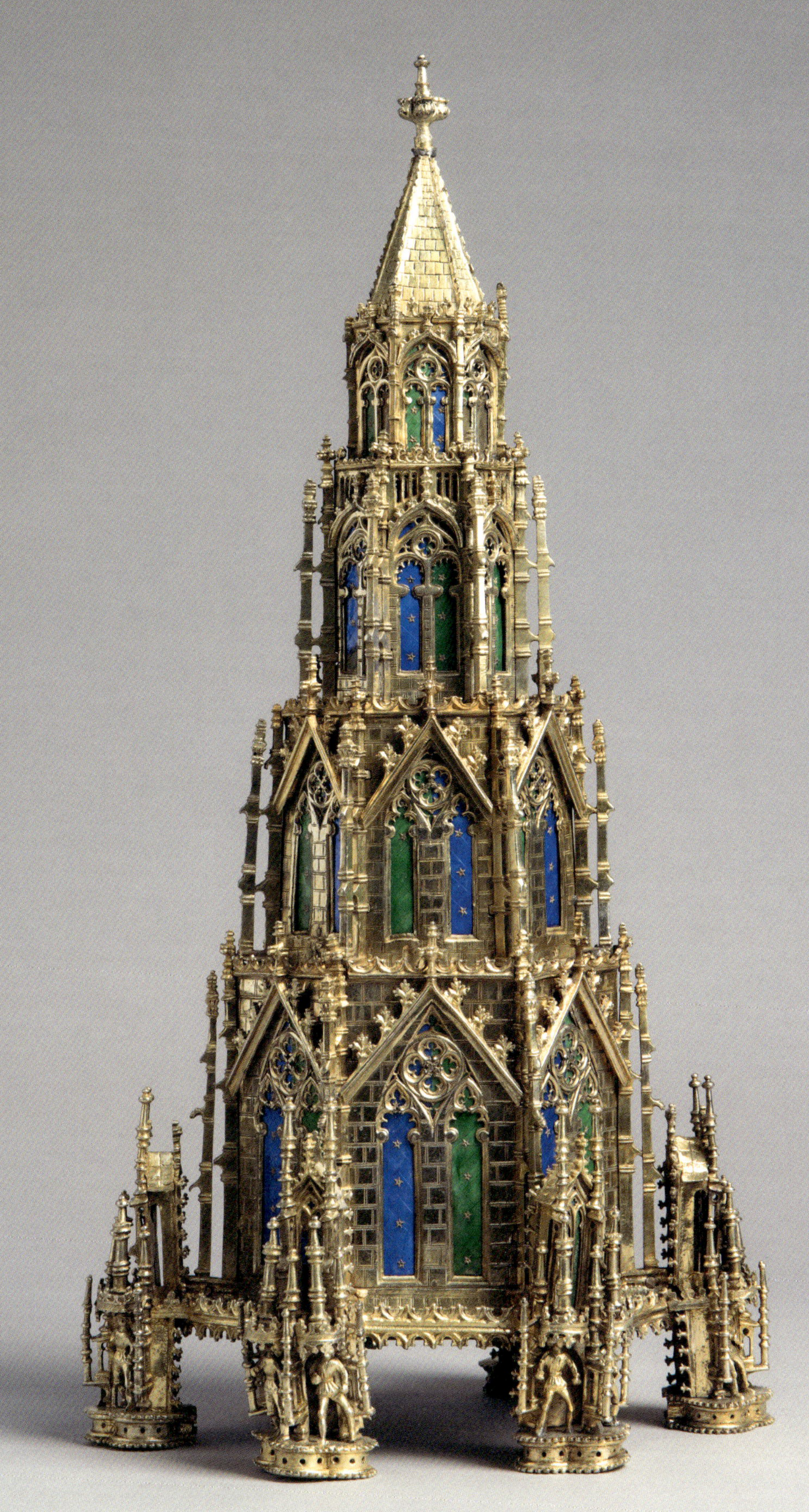

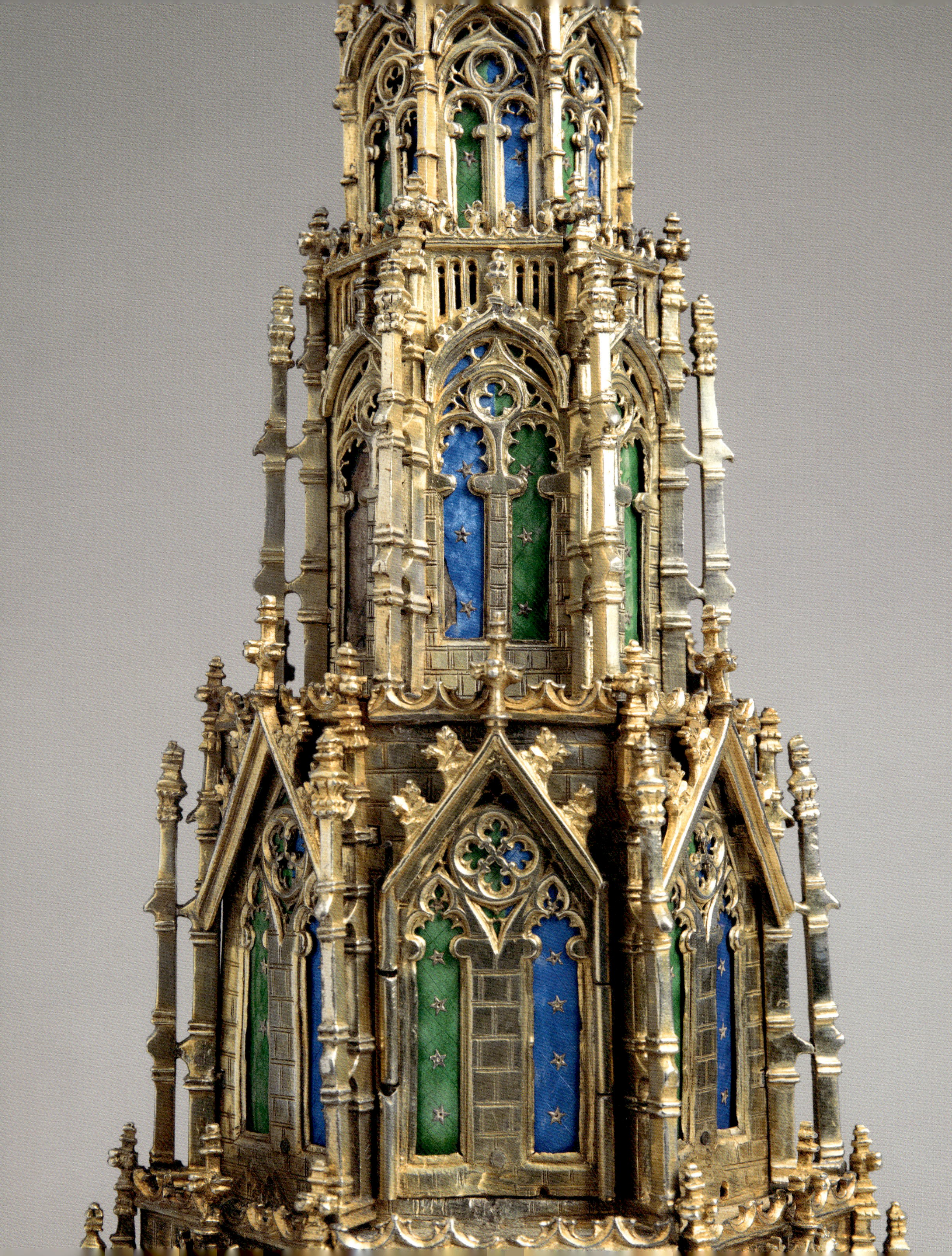

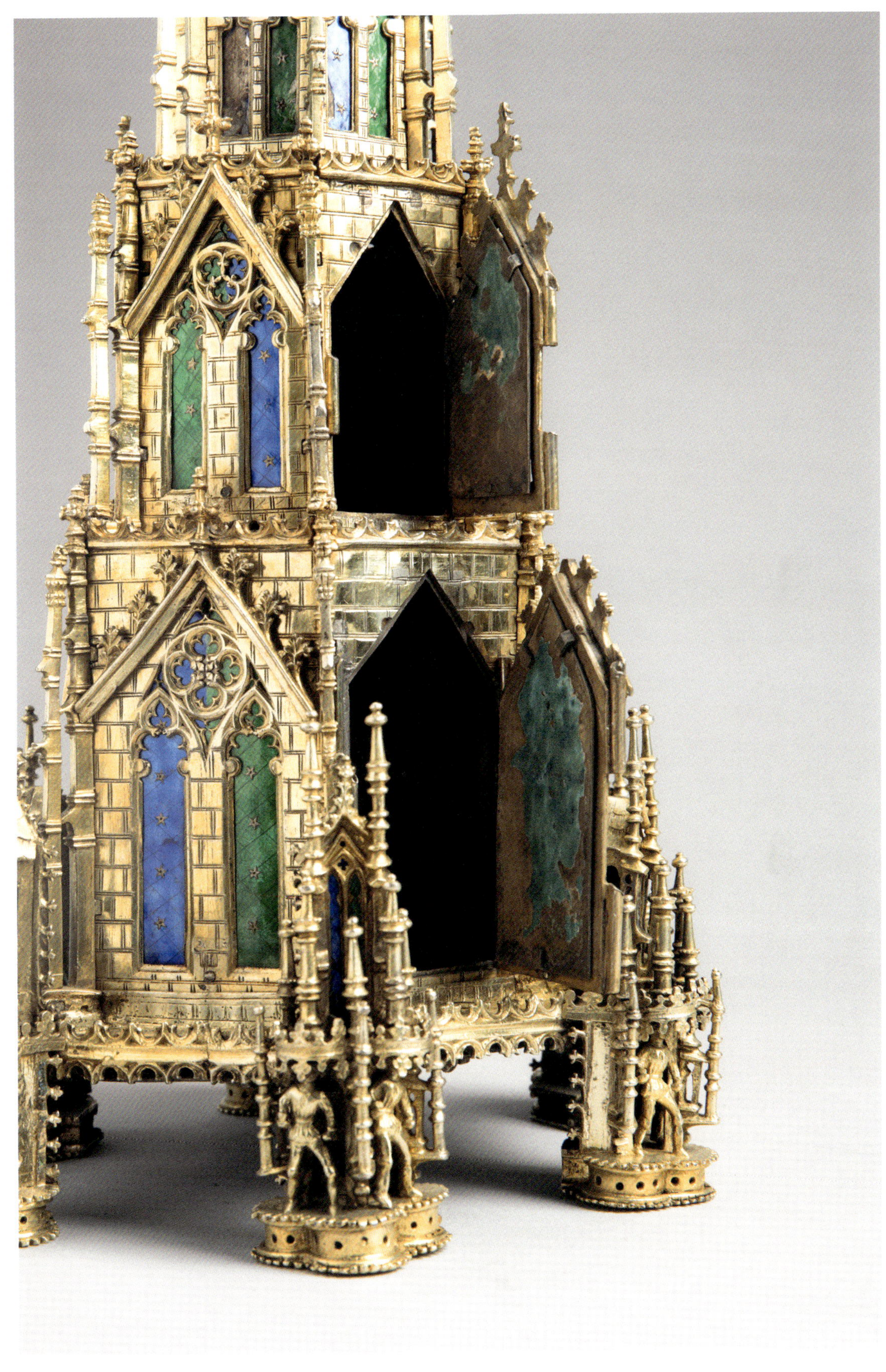

17

PAOLO DA VISSO (active 1431–1482)
The Crucifixion, attended by a Franciscan Monk
Italy, Le Marche, Aschio
*c.*1450
42 × 30.2 × 3 cm / 16.5 × 11.9 × 1 in.
Tempera and gold on panel

PROVENANCE
Sterbini Collection, Rome
Private collection, Switzerland

PUBLISHED
Venturi (1906), page 86–89; Zeri (1976), page 51–54.

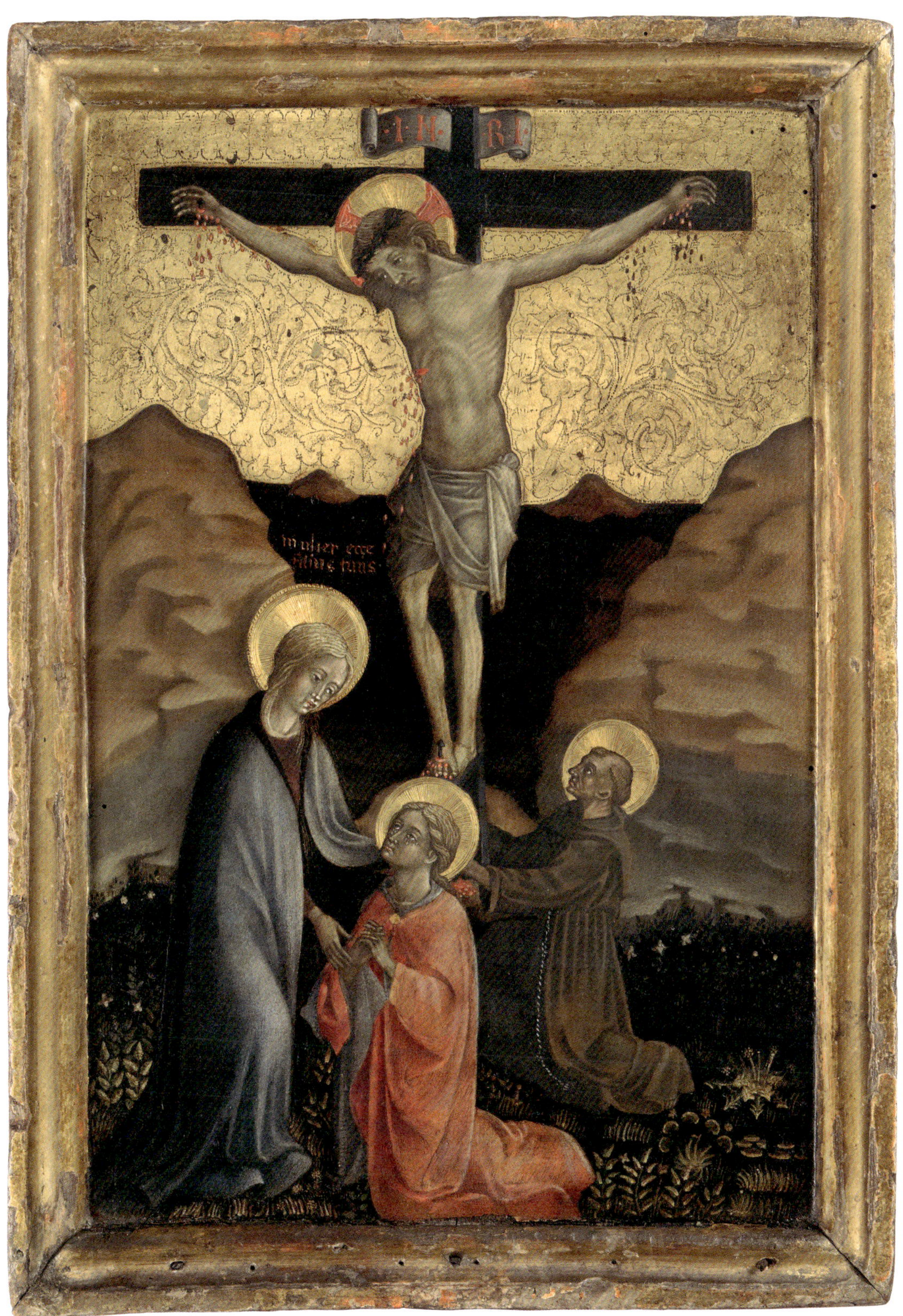
INRI
mulier ecce
filius tuus

18

An onyx cameo of René of Anjou (1409–1480)
France
*c.*1470
2.1 × 1.8 cm / 0.8 × 0.7 in. (cameo)
Onyx cameo set in a modern gold ring, impeccable
condition

PROVENANCE
Commissioned by René of Anjou for his court; August
Merklein Collection, Nuremberg (1865–1940); thence
by descent.

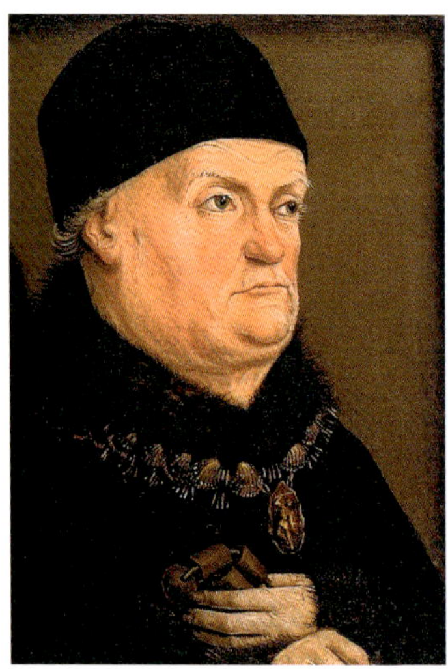

Nicolas Froment (1430–1484), *Portrait of
René of Anjou* (*c.*1475)

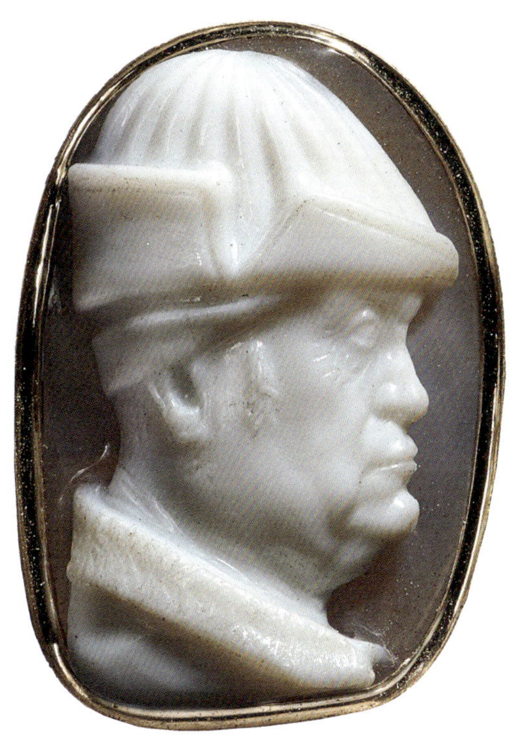

Work scale

19

THE COËTIVY MASTER (HENRI DE VULCOP?),
(active *c.*1450–1485)

A Book of Hours, for the Use of Paris, in Latin and French

France, Paris or the Loire Valley
*c.*1470s
11.2 × 8.2 cm / 4.4 × 3.2 in.
Illuminated manuscript with ink, pigments and gold leaf on vellum, in a late sixteenth-century Parisian dark brown morocco binding gilt à la fanfare, 288 leaves richly illuminated with 9 full-page miniatures and 9 historiated initials

PROVENANCE
Sotheby's, 12 July 1971, lot 56; Collection of Arthur Haddaway (1901–1981); Christie's New York, 25 September 1981, lot 8; H.P. Kraus, 1982; Rosenberg collection, until 2021.

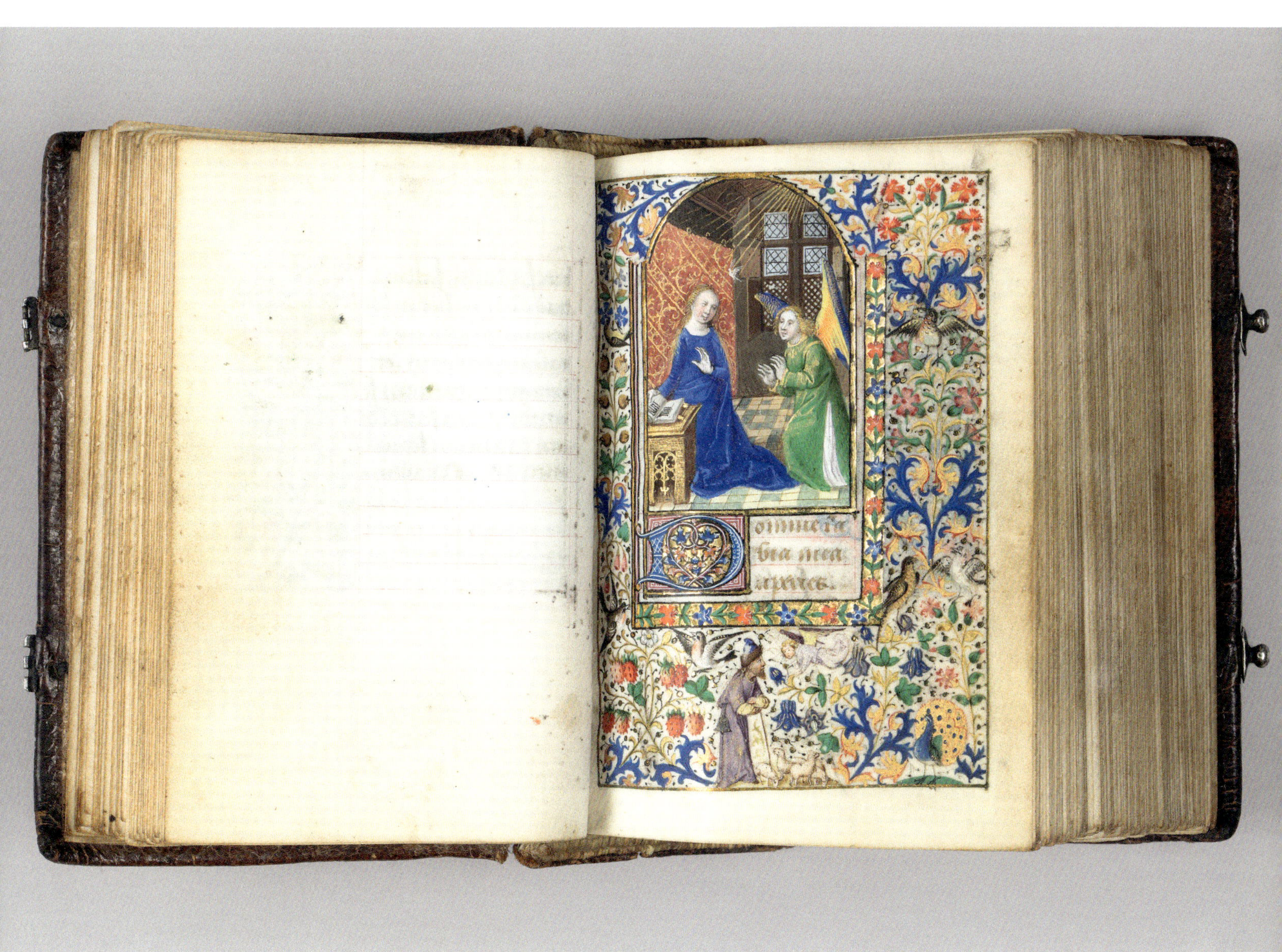
Domine la
bia mea
aperies.

Illi autem prophete
predicauerunt vbiq[ue]
domino cooperante z
sermone confirmante
sequentib[us] signis.
Deo gratias.

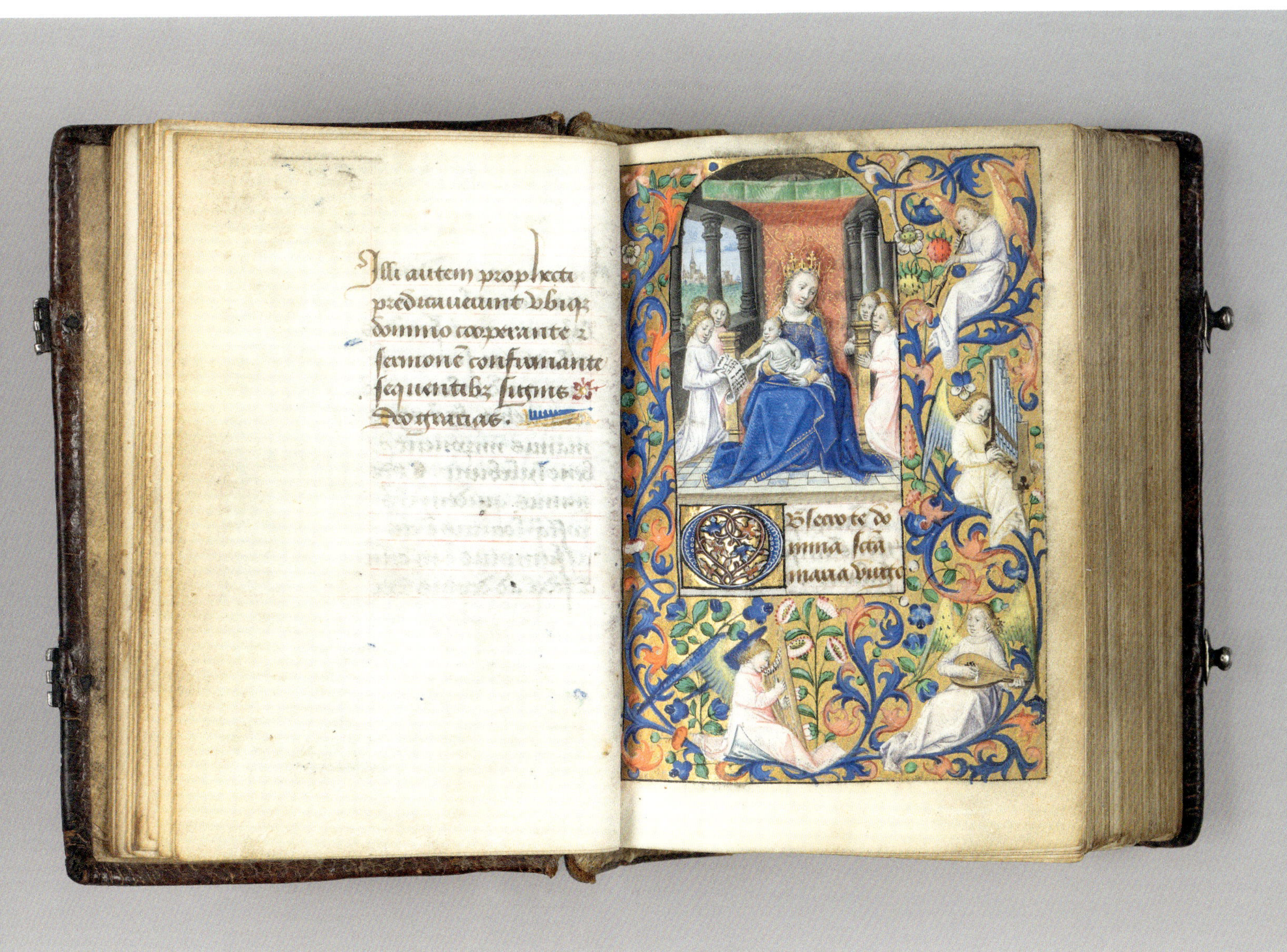

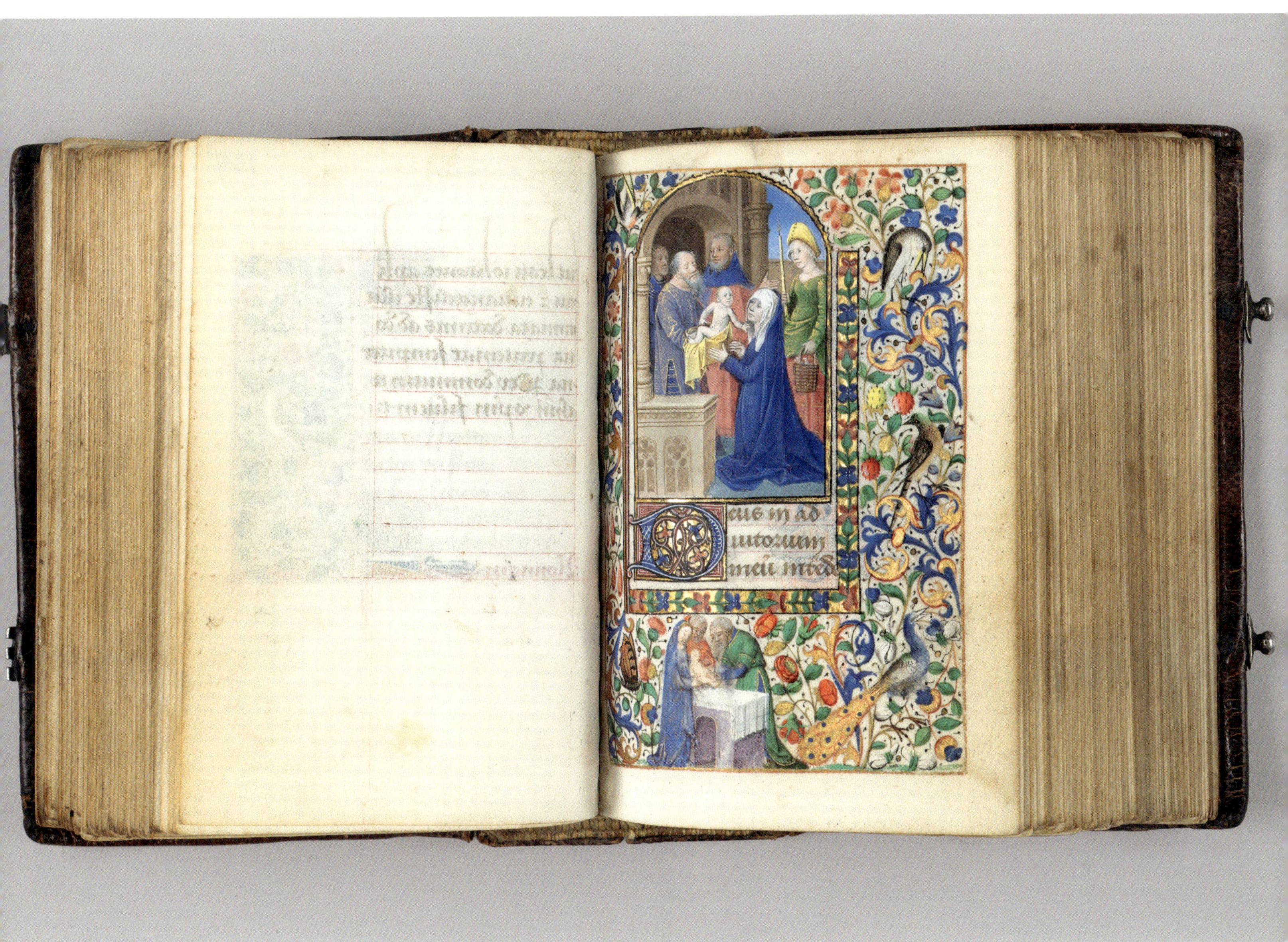

Deus in ad-
iutorium
meum inten[de]

20

FERNANDO GALLEGO (Salamanca, 1440–1507)
**Triptych of the Virgin and Child with Saints
Andrew, John, Catherine and Eustace**
*c.*1480–1490
Central panel 67 × 44.8 × 2.8 cm / 26.4 × 17.6 × 1 in.;
each wing 66.8 × 22.5 × 2.7 cm / 26.25 × 8.75 × 1 in.
Oil and gilding on softwood panels with original split
hinges and applied framing elements, imitation of
porphyry on reverse

PROVENANCE
Collection of Leo Spik, 1968; Private collection, Berlin,
1968–2019; Sold by the heirs through Leo Spik, Berlin,
3rd December 2020, lot 211.

PUBLISHED
Maroto, (2020), 66–75.

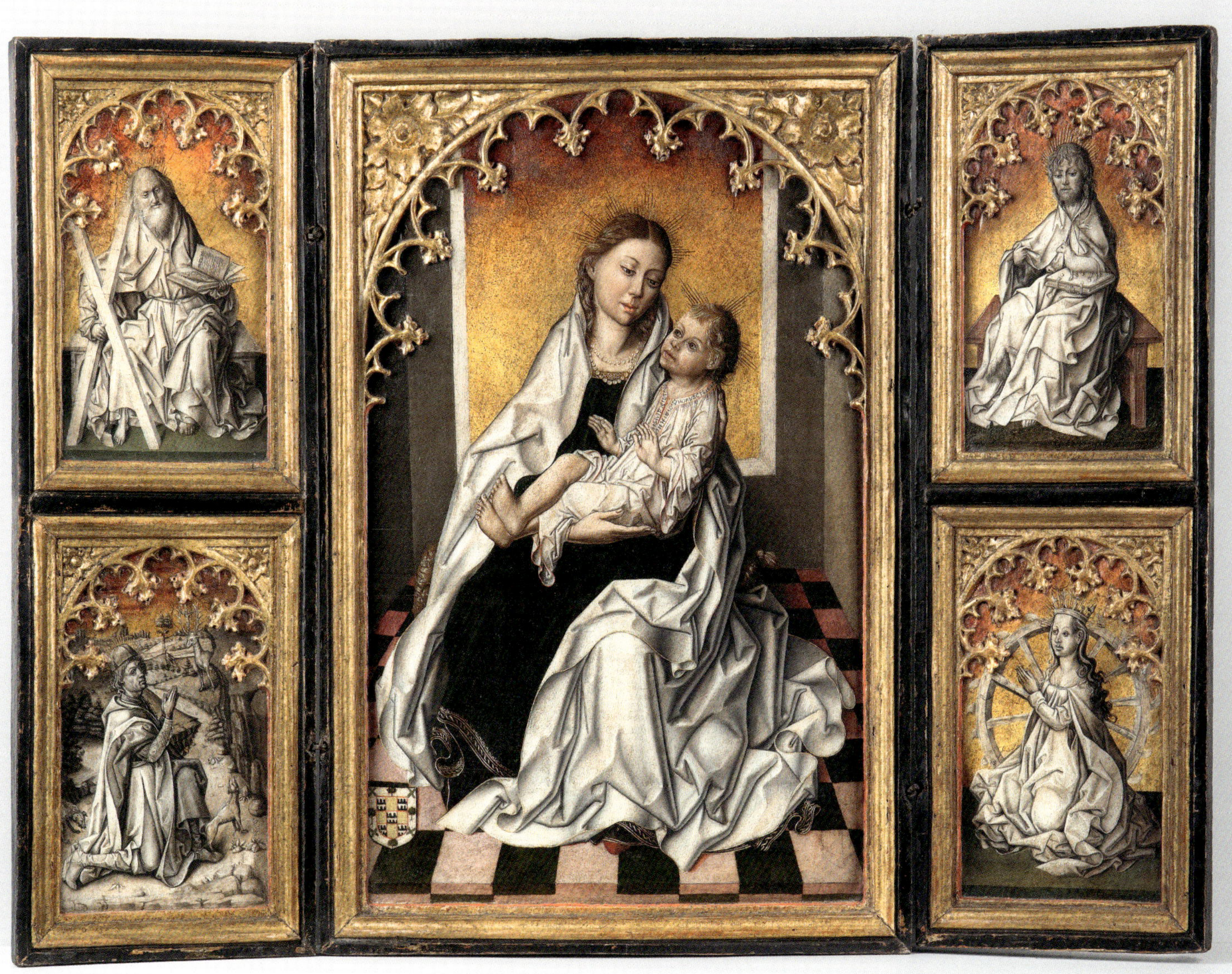

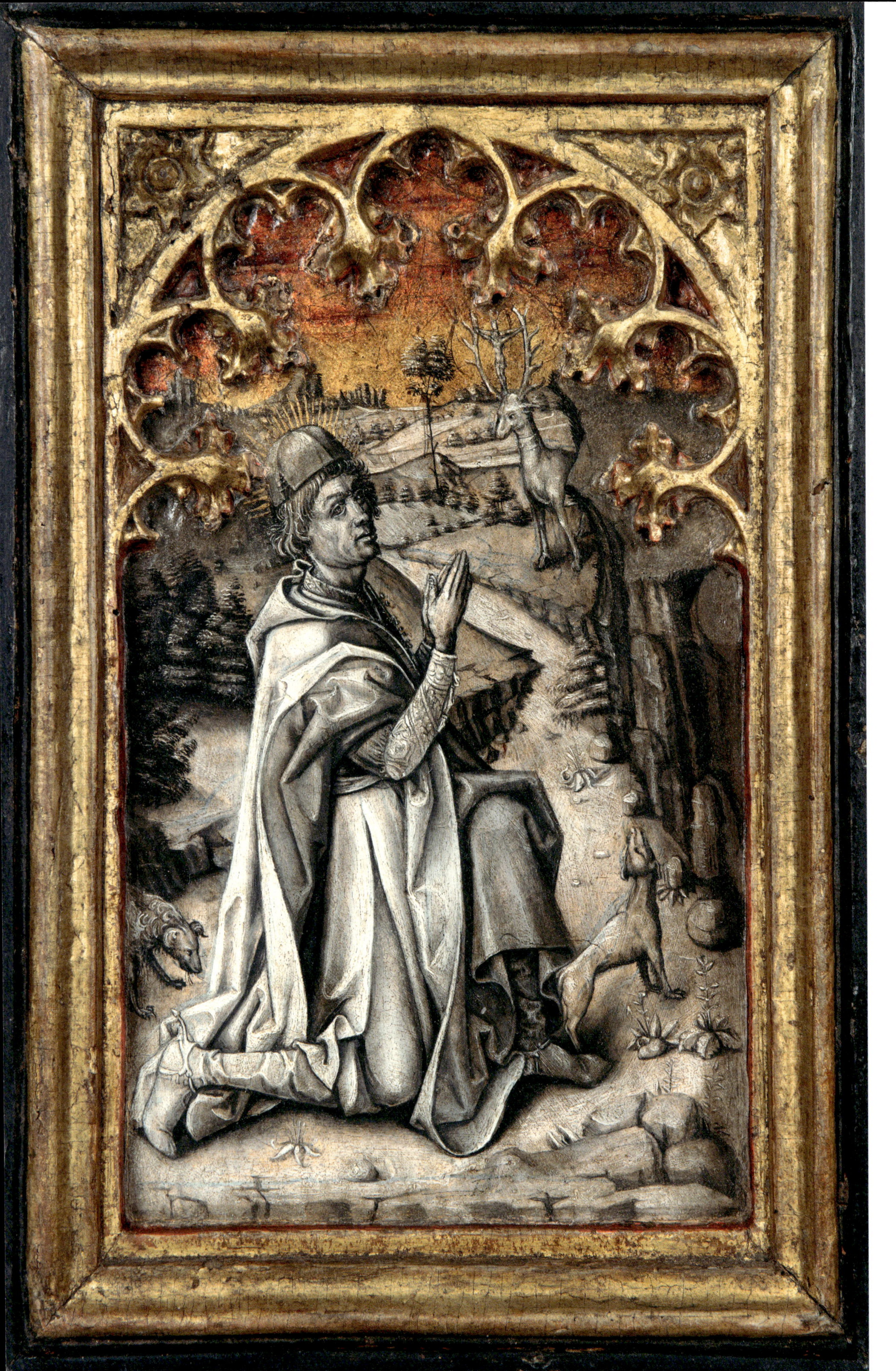

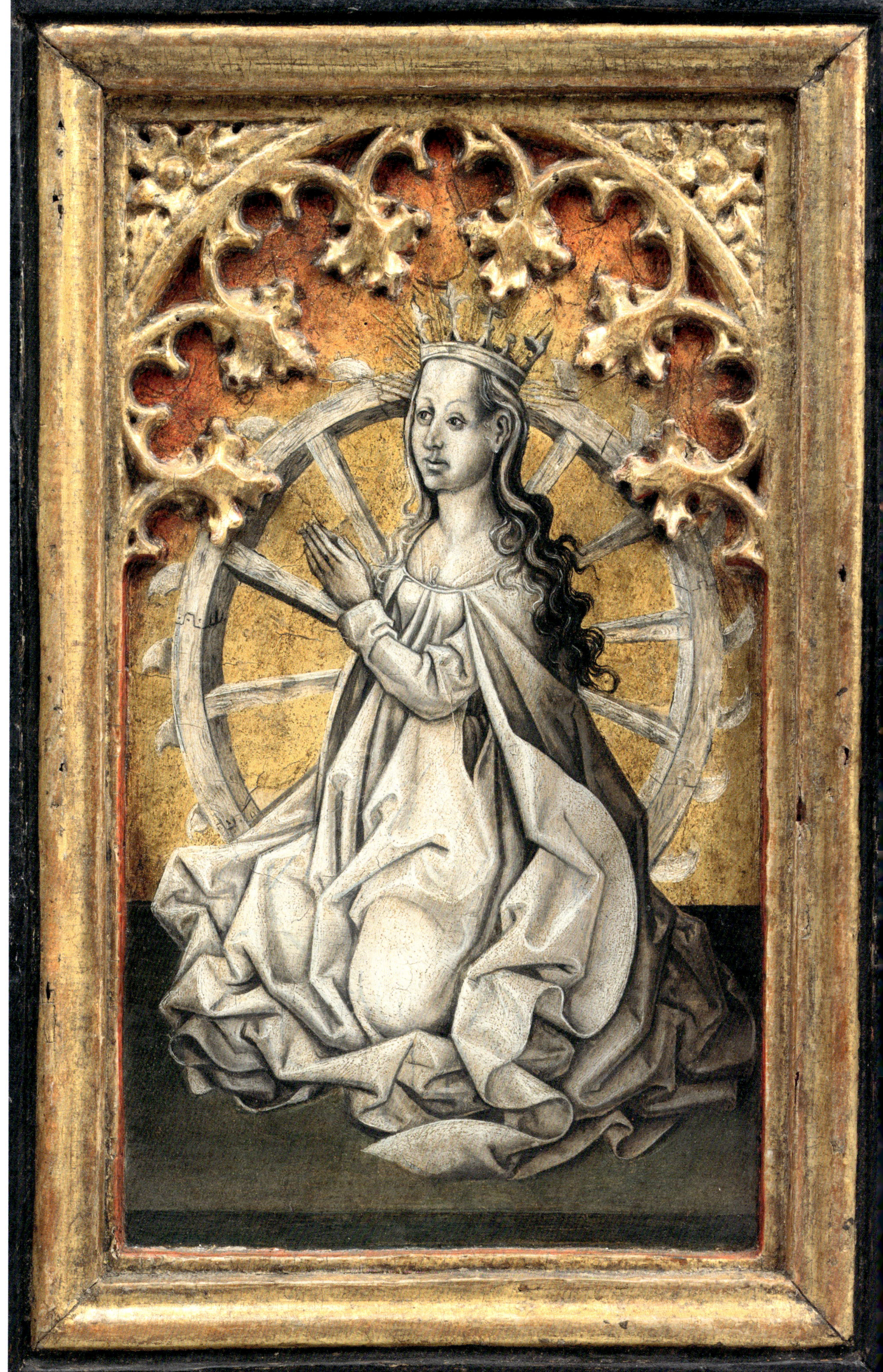

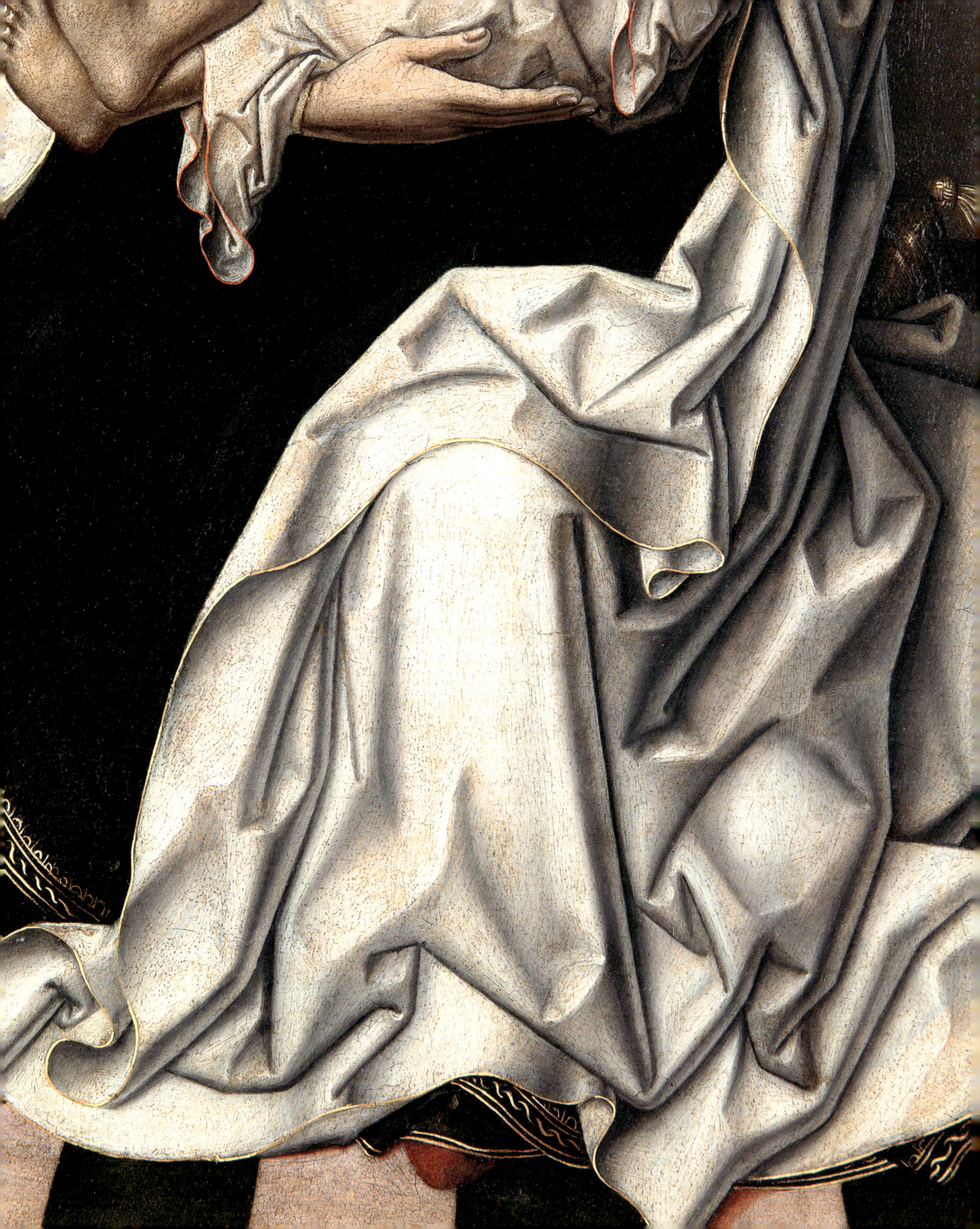

21

HANS GREIFF (active c.1470, d.1516)?
A monumental lidded cup with the figure of a courtier and three soldiers
Germany, Bavaria, Ingolstadt
c.1470
55 cm / 21.7 in. (height) × 18.8 cm / 7.4 in.
(diameter at widest point); cast, hammered, chased
and gilded silver

PROVENANCE
The Portland Collection, Welbeck Abbey, by 1854;
By descent until 2021.

PUBLISHED
Harcourt House Inventory (1854); Jones (1935).

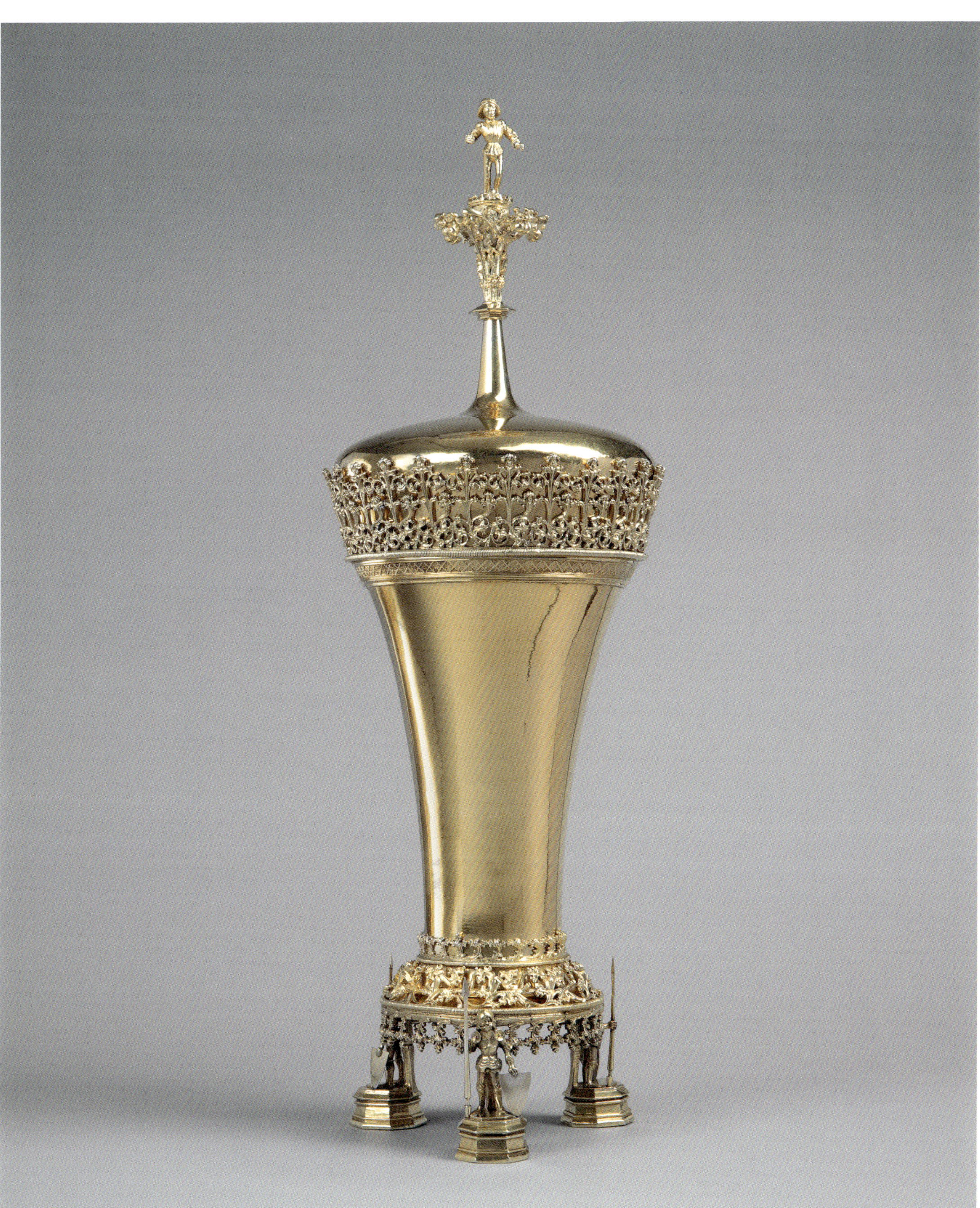

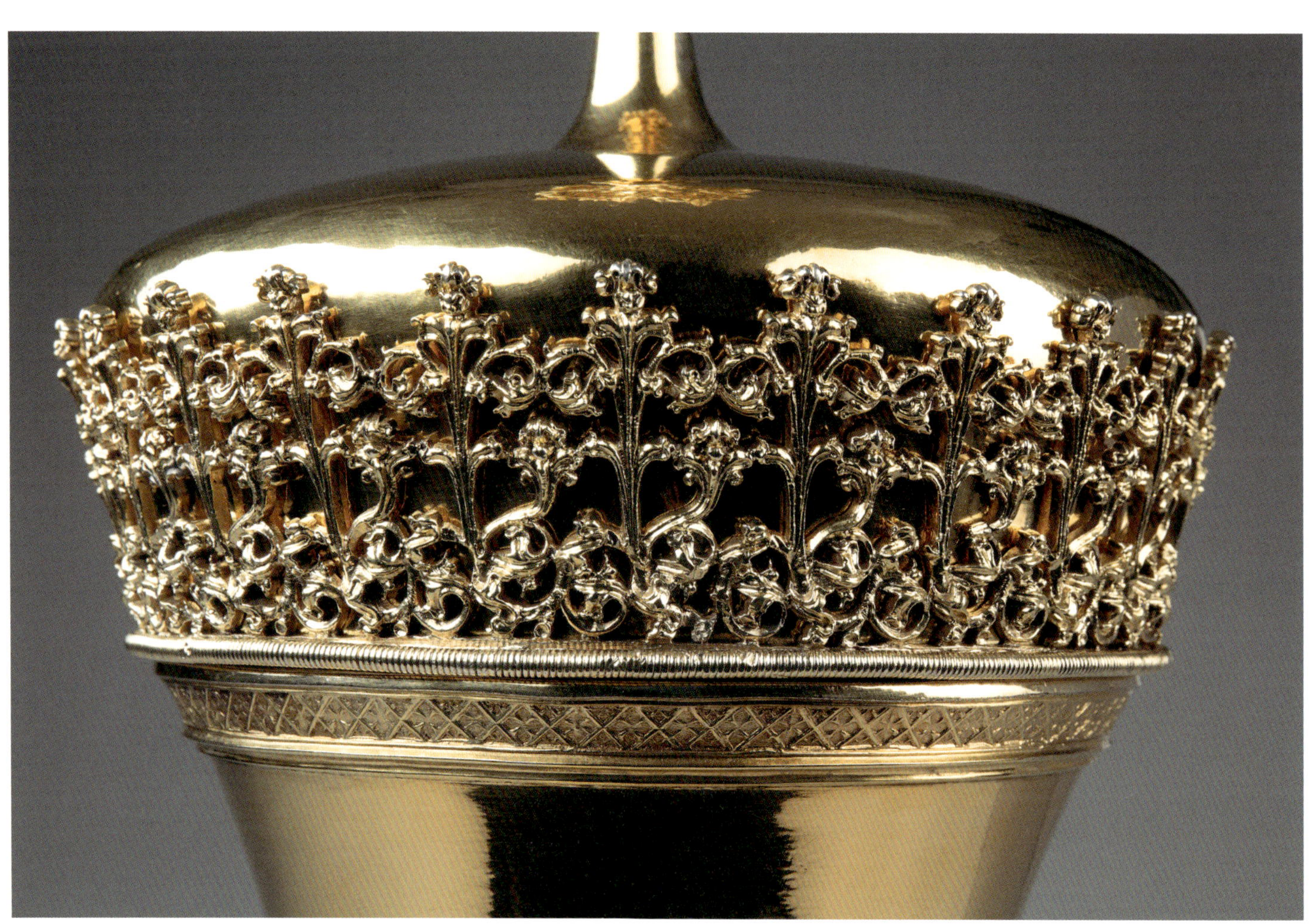

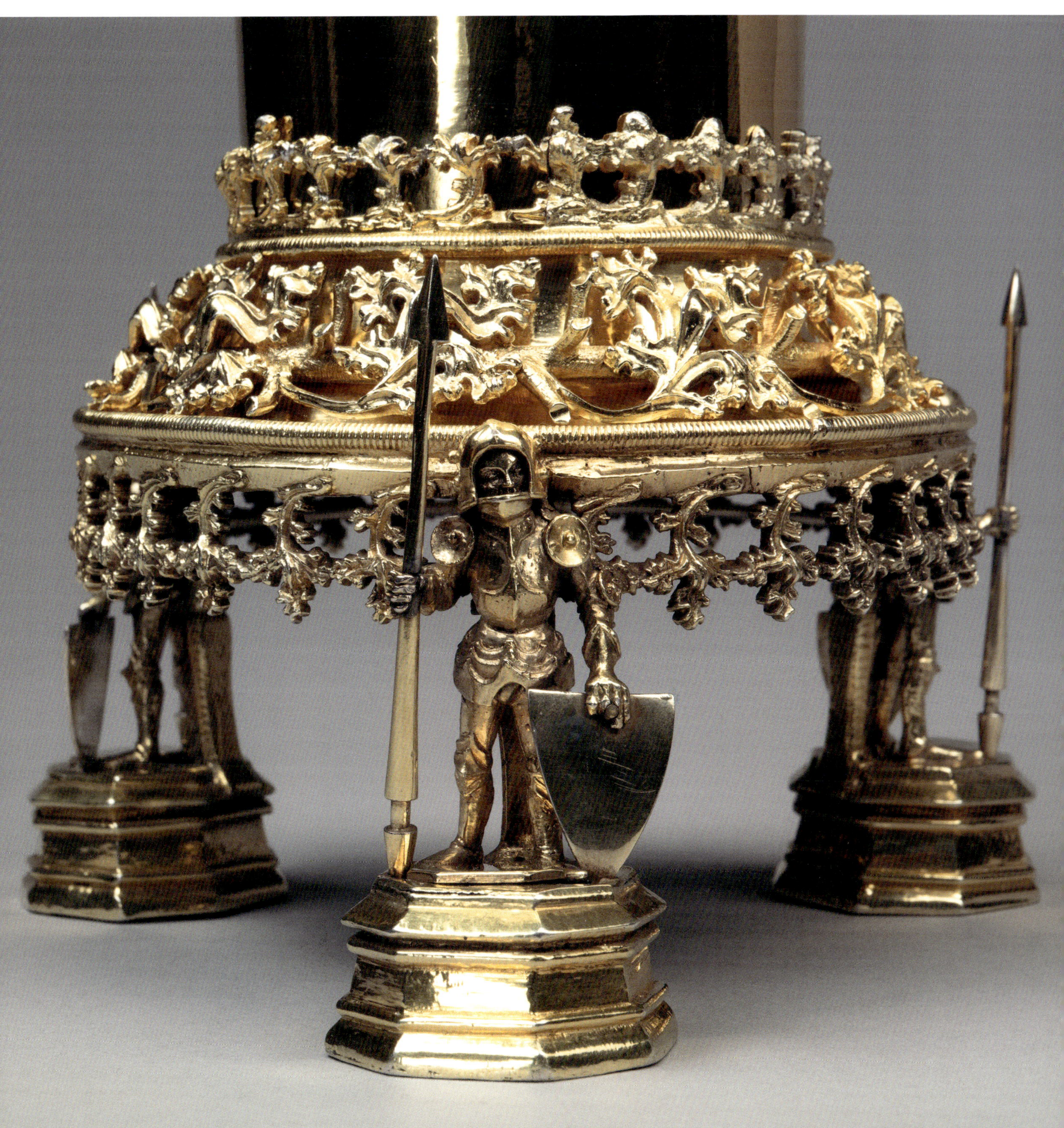

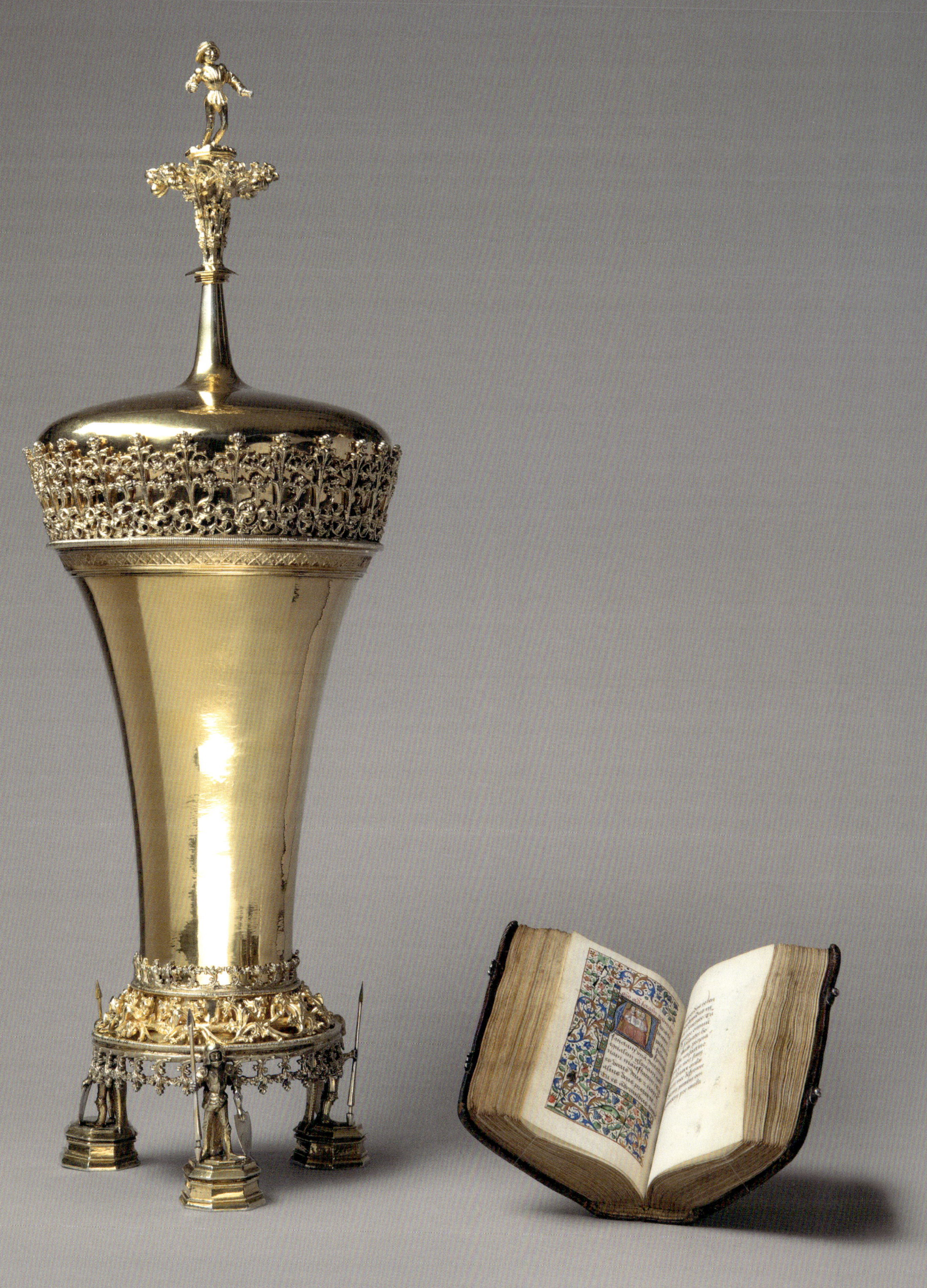

LORENZ LECHLER (c.1460–1538) **AND WORKSHOP**
Monumental Drawing of a Sacrament House
Southwestern Germany
Dated 1502
323 × 36.5 cm / 127 × 14.4 in.; a design for a colossal architectural
structure estimated to have been around 70 feet tall, in ink on
three joined sheets of parchment, with some 85 drawings for
sculpted figures and scenes

PROVENANCE
The Princely collection of Öettingen-Wallerstein, Harburg Castle,
by c.1820; acquired directly from the above in 2017.

Work scale

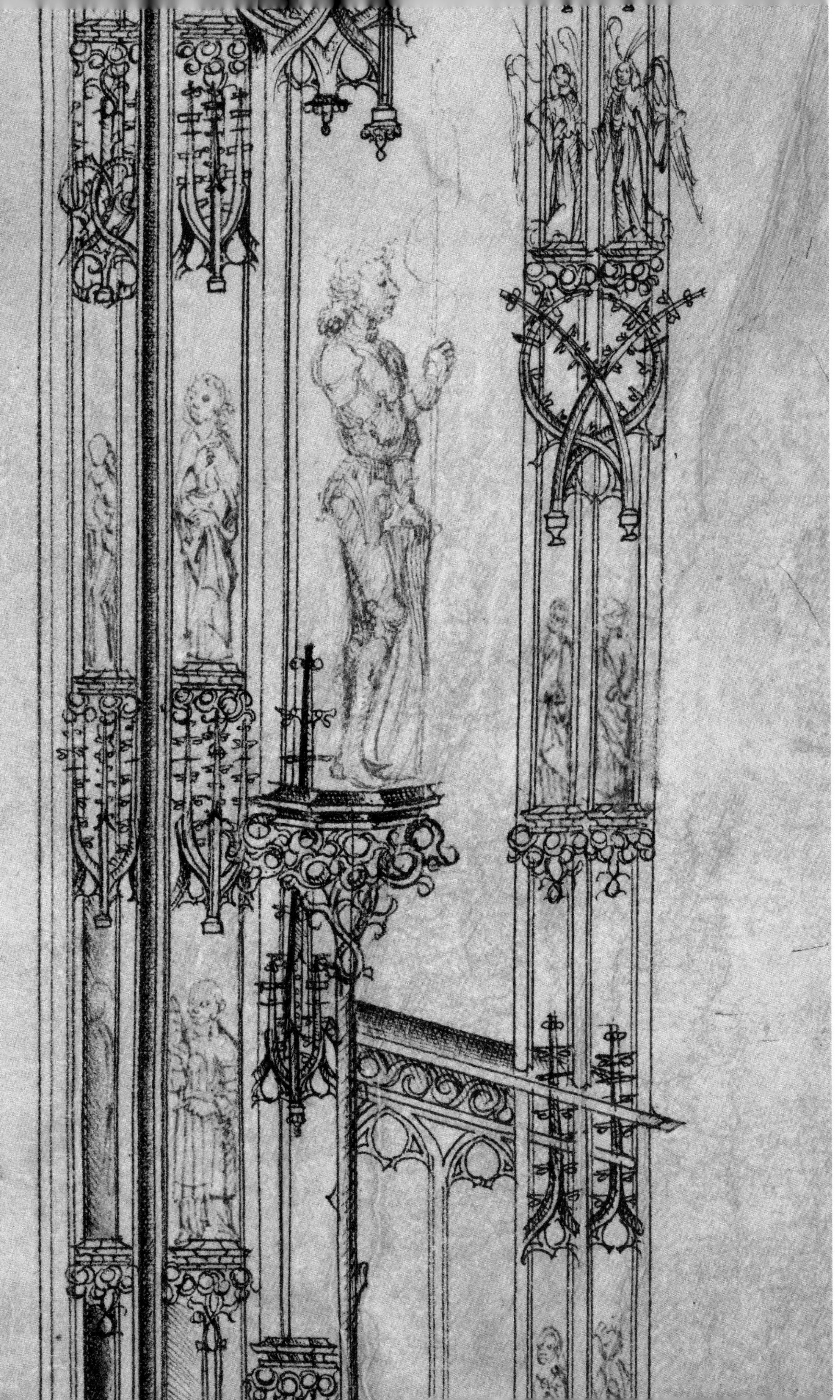

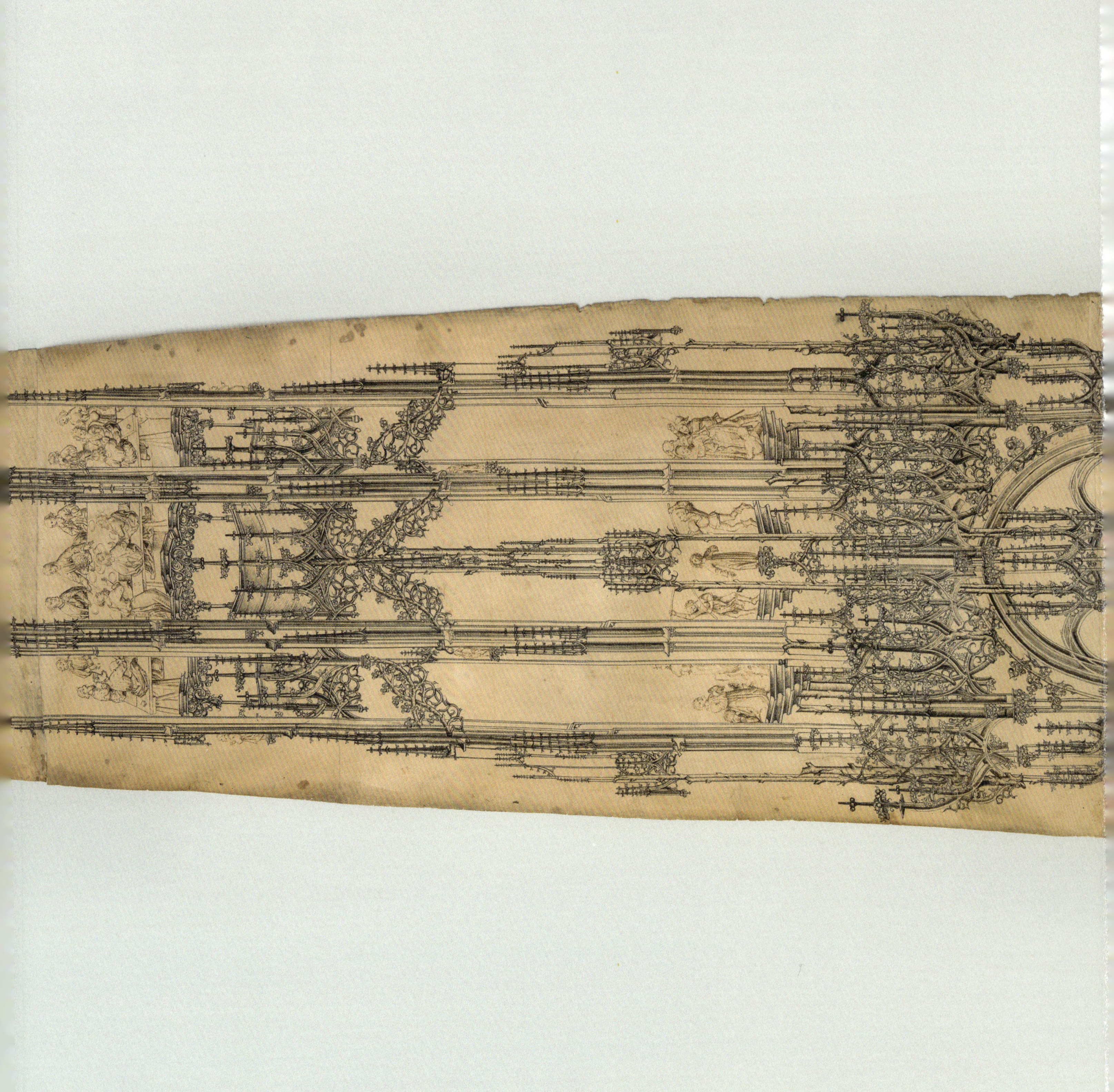

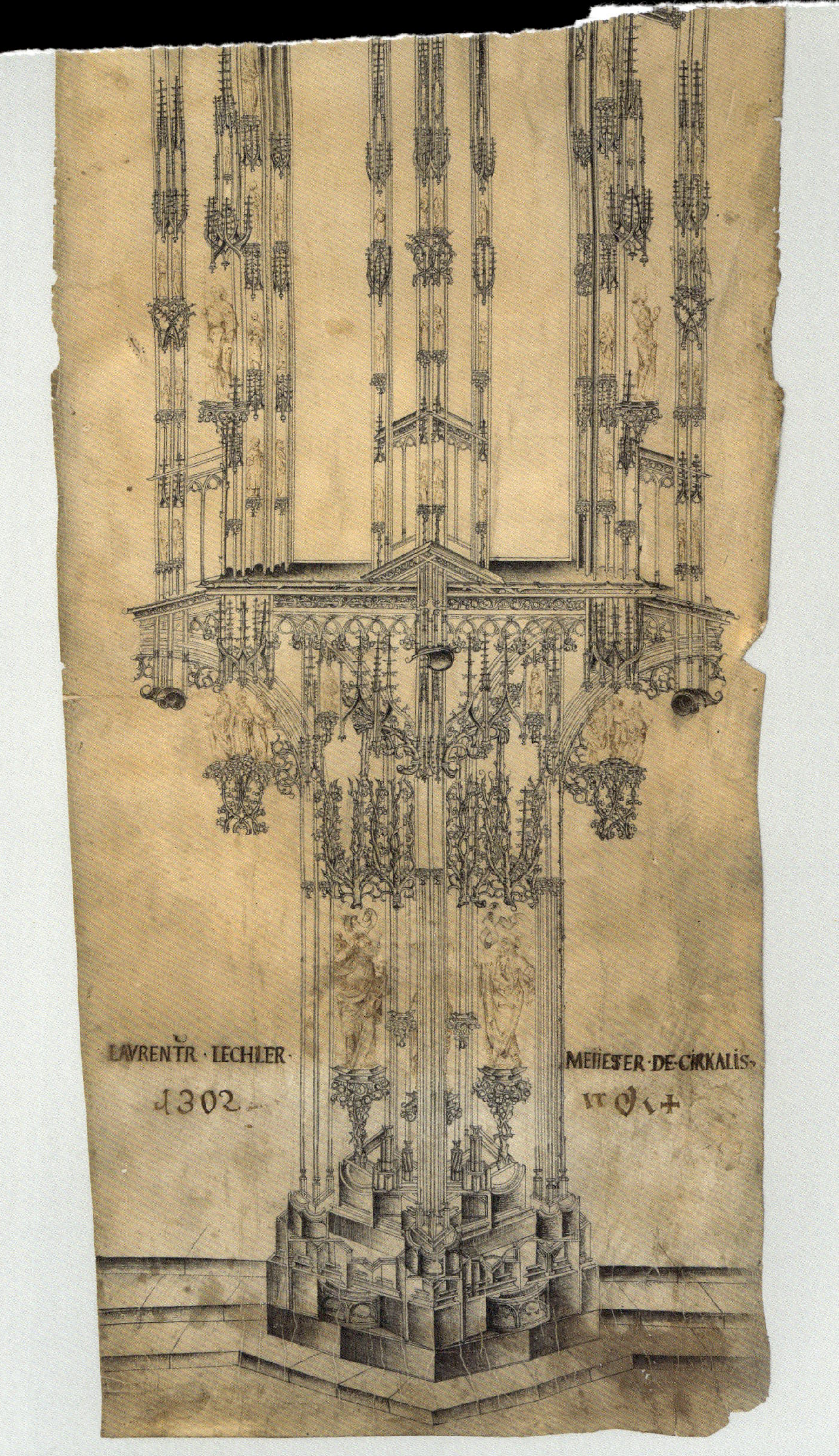
LAVRENTR·LECHLER
1302
MEIISTER·DE·CIRKALIS·
IT O ı +

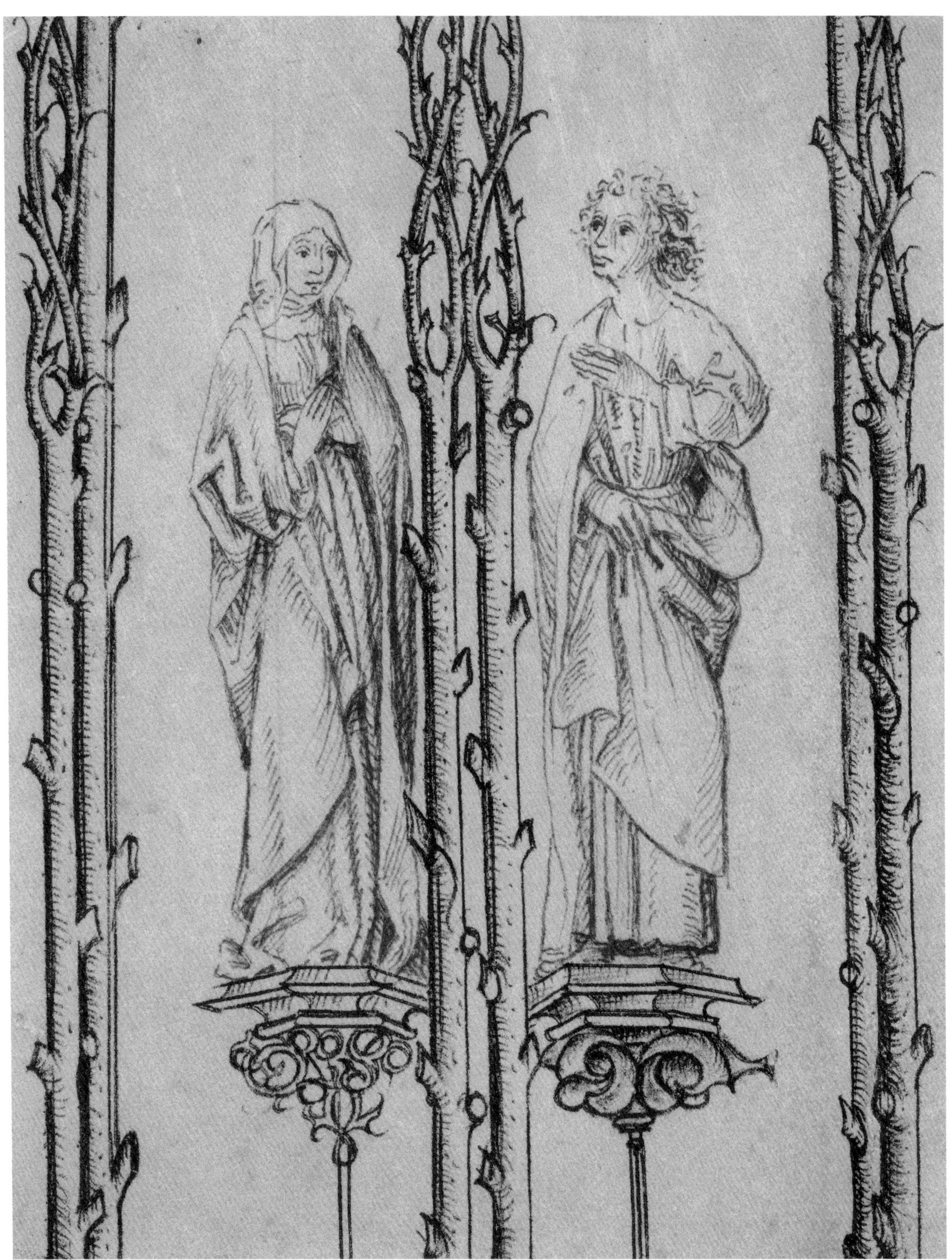

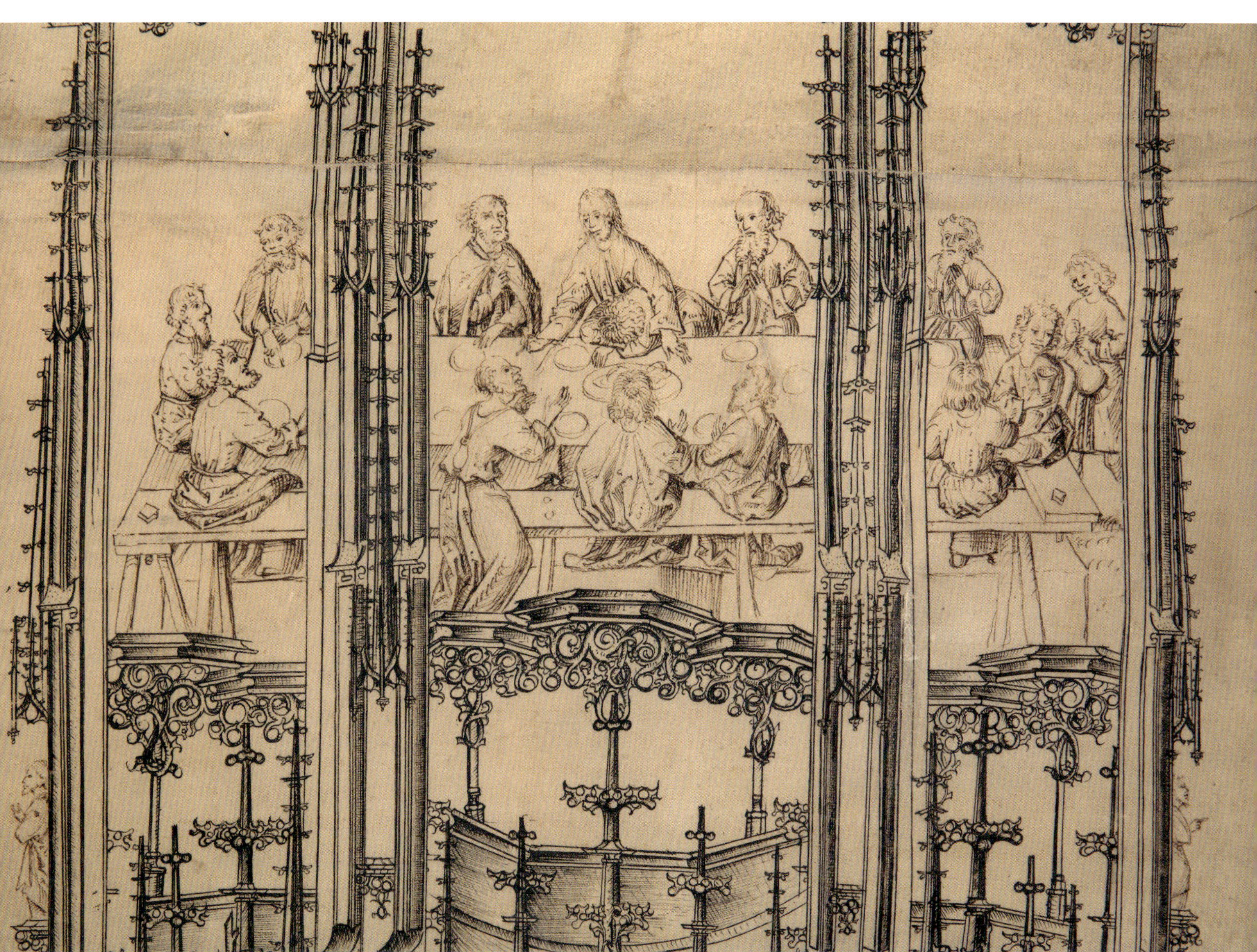

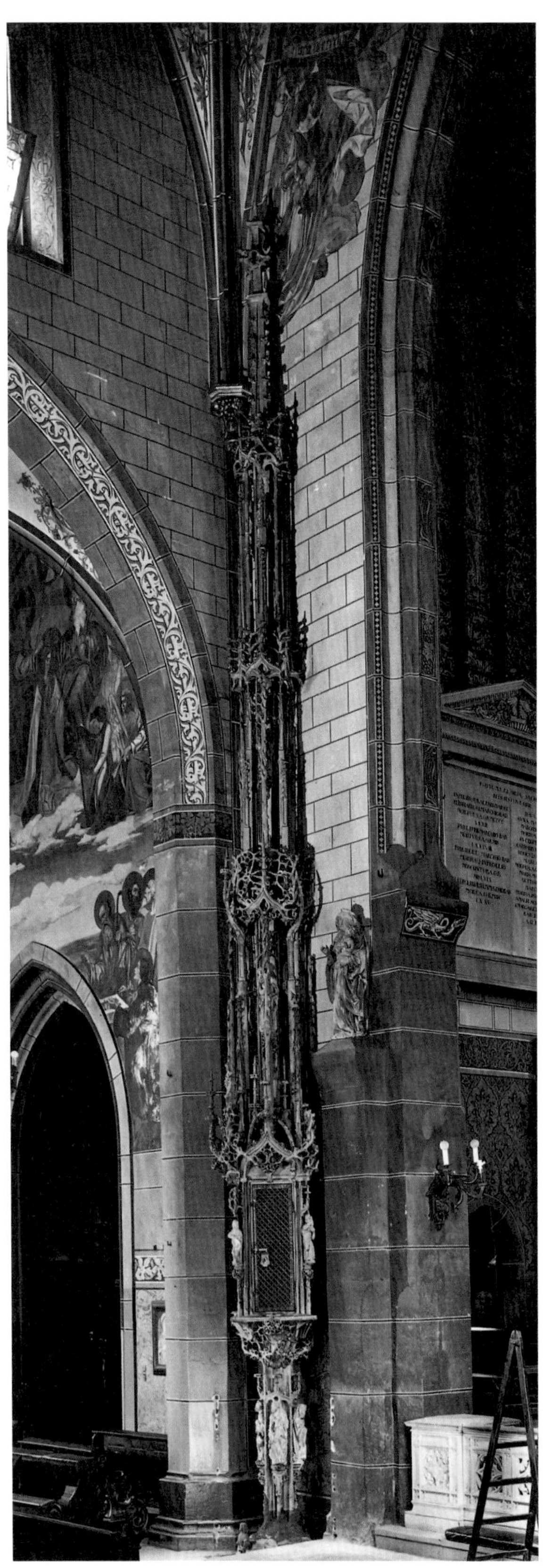

Lechler Workshop, Tabernacle in Baden-Baden
(Photo: Wilhelm Kratt. Karlsruhe Archive, c.1910)

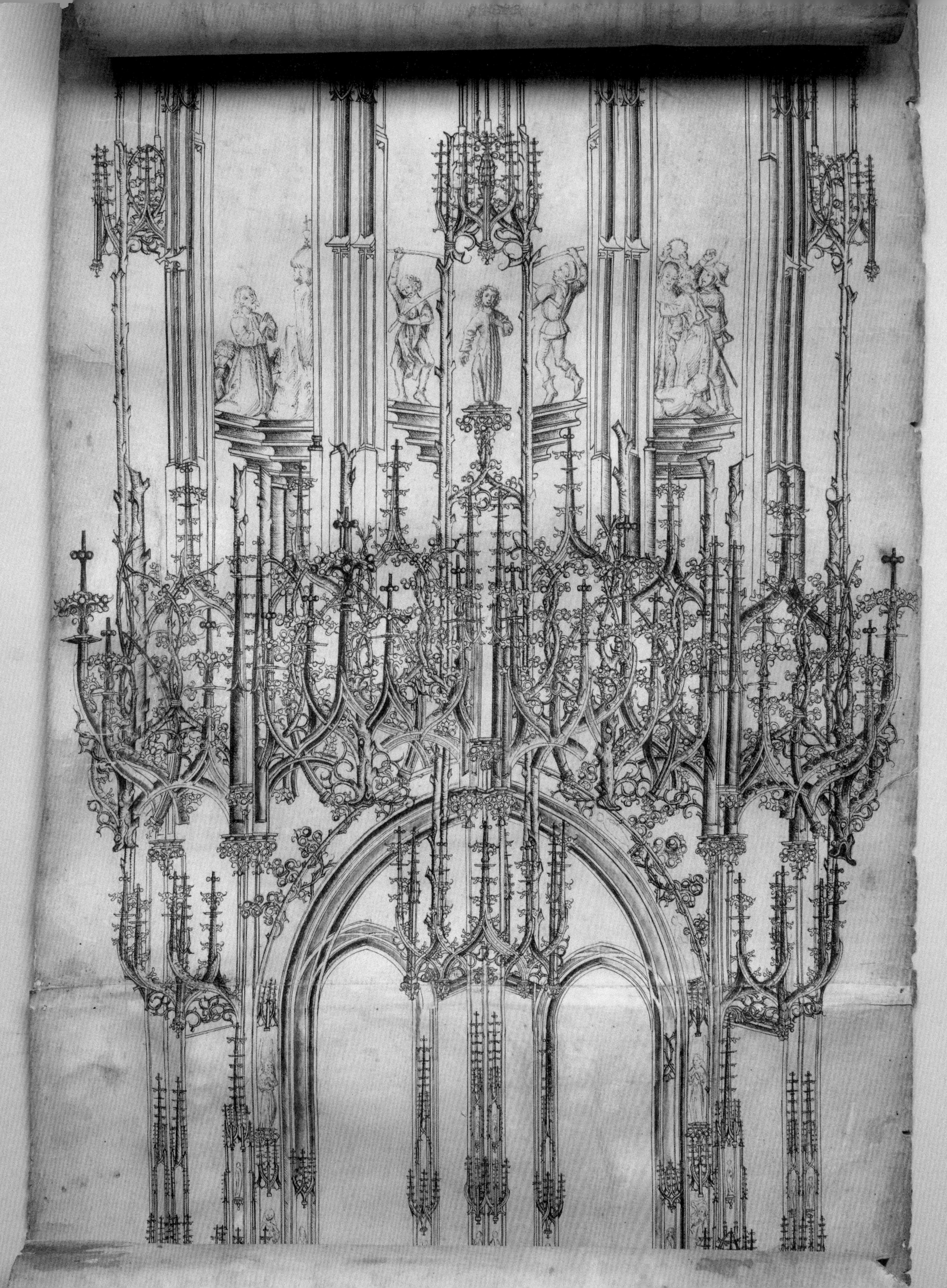

23

The Death of the Virgin
Germany, Lower Rhine, Kalkar
*c.*1490
73 × 110 cm / 28.7 × 43.3 in.
Oak

PROVENANCE
Flemish private collection

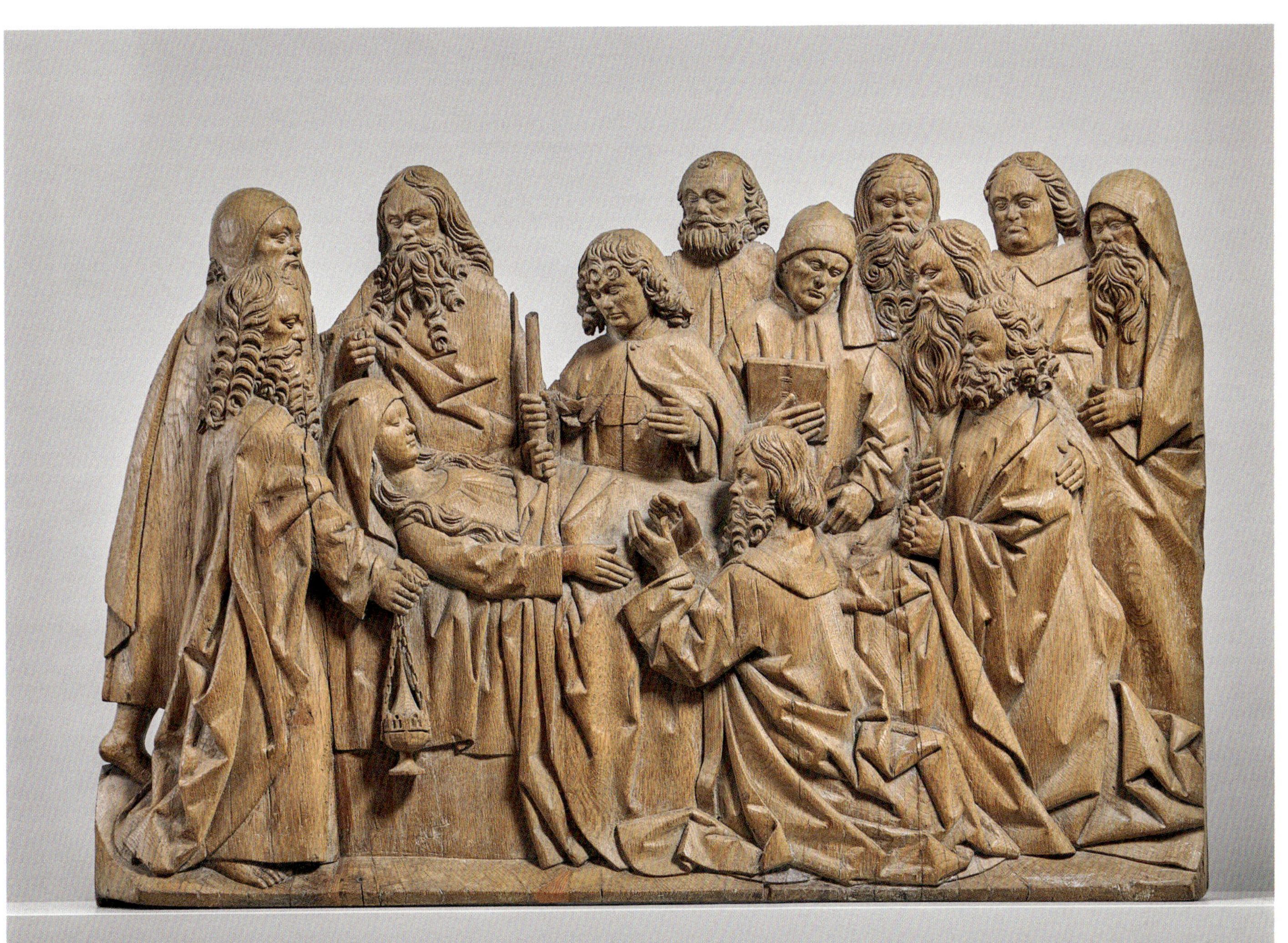

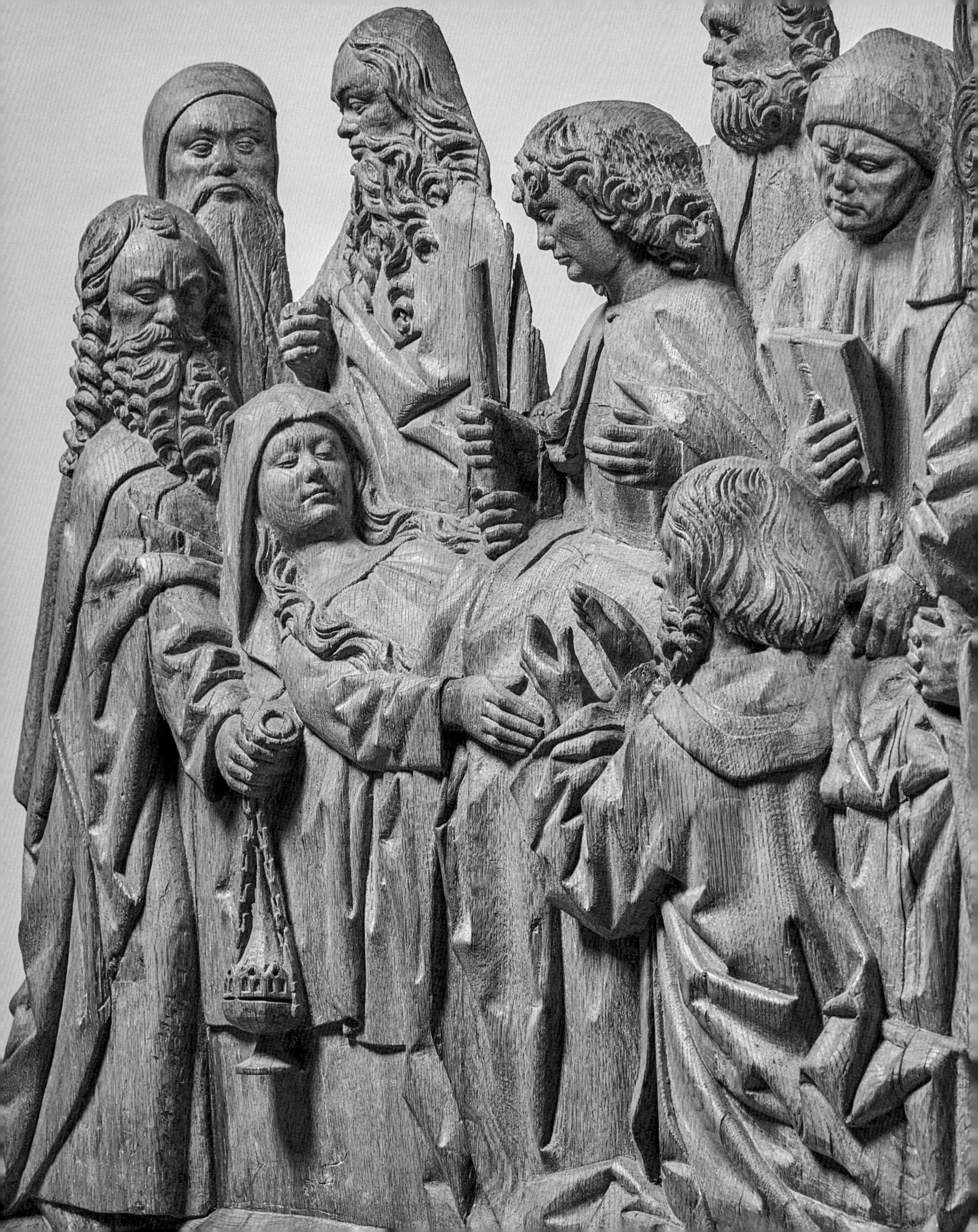

24

JÖRG LEDERER (*c.*1470–1550)
Saint Sebastian
Southern Germany, Kaufbeuren
*c.*1515–1520
116 × 76 × 38 cm / 45.7 × 30 × 15 in.
Fully polychromed and gilded in limewood

PROVENANCE
Österreichisches Galerie, Vienna (inventory #5426),
acquired June 30, 1921 and deaccessioned July 1922;
With Treuga AG, acquired from the above July 1922;
Auktionshaus für Altertümer Glückselig, Vienna,
May 4/5, 1925, lot 64 (as South German, circa 1535);
Austrian Noble Collection; Blumka Gallery & Julius
Böhler, New York and Starnberg;
Collection of Hester Diamond, acquired 2018.

PUBLISHED
Husband (2017).

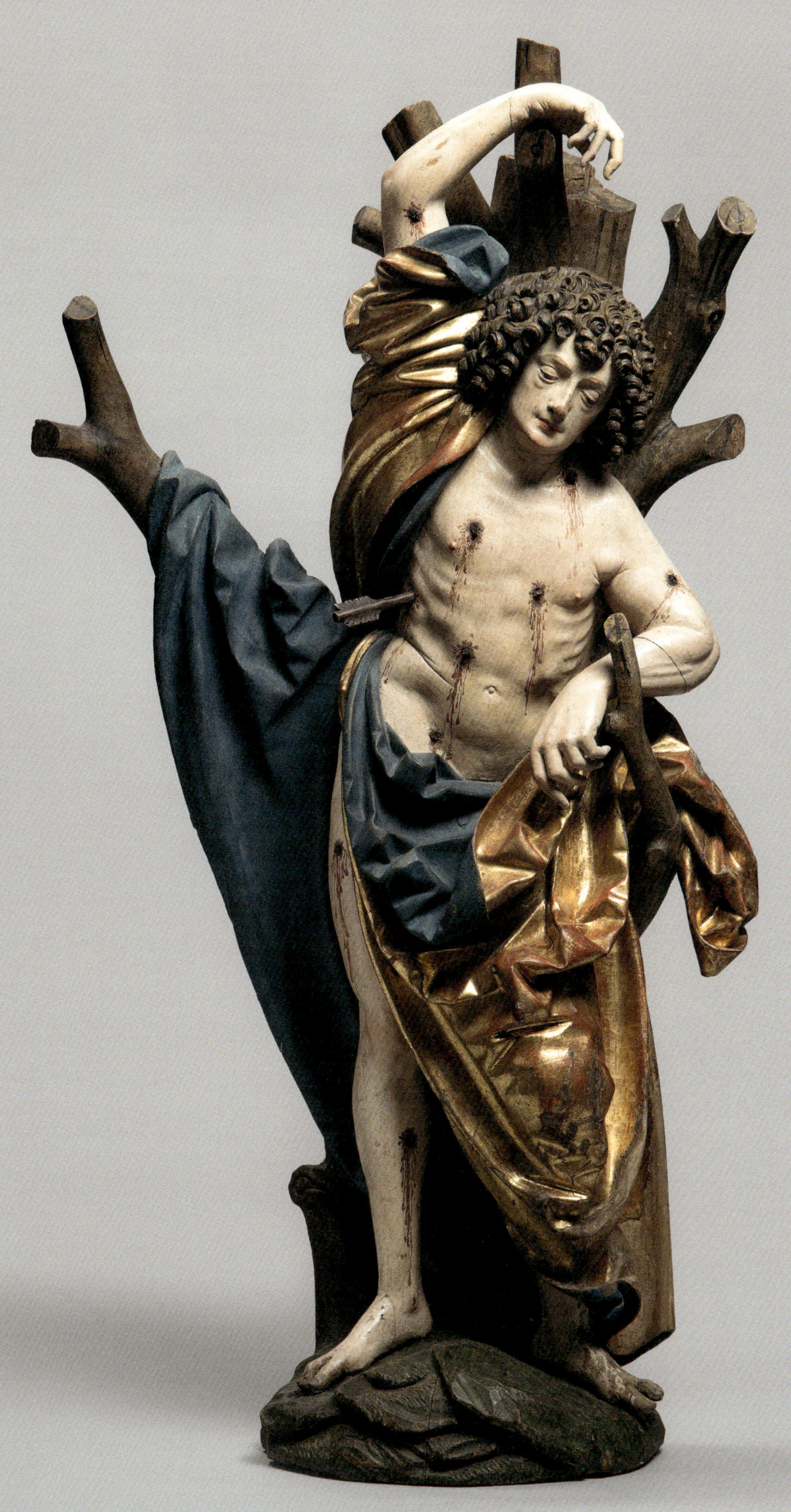

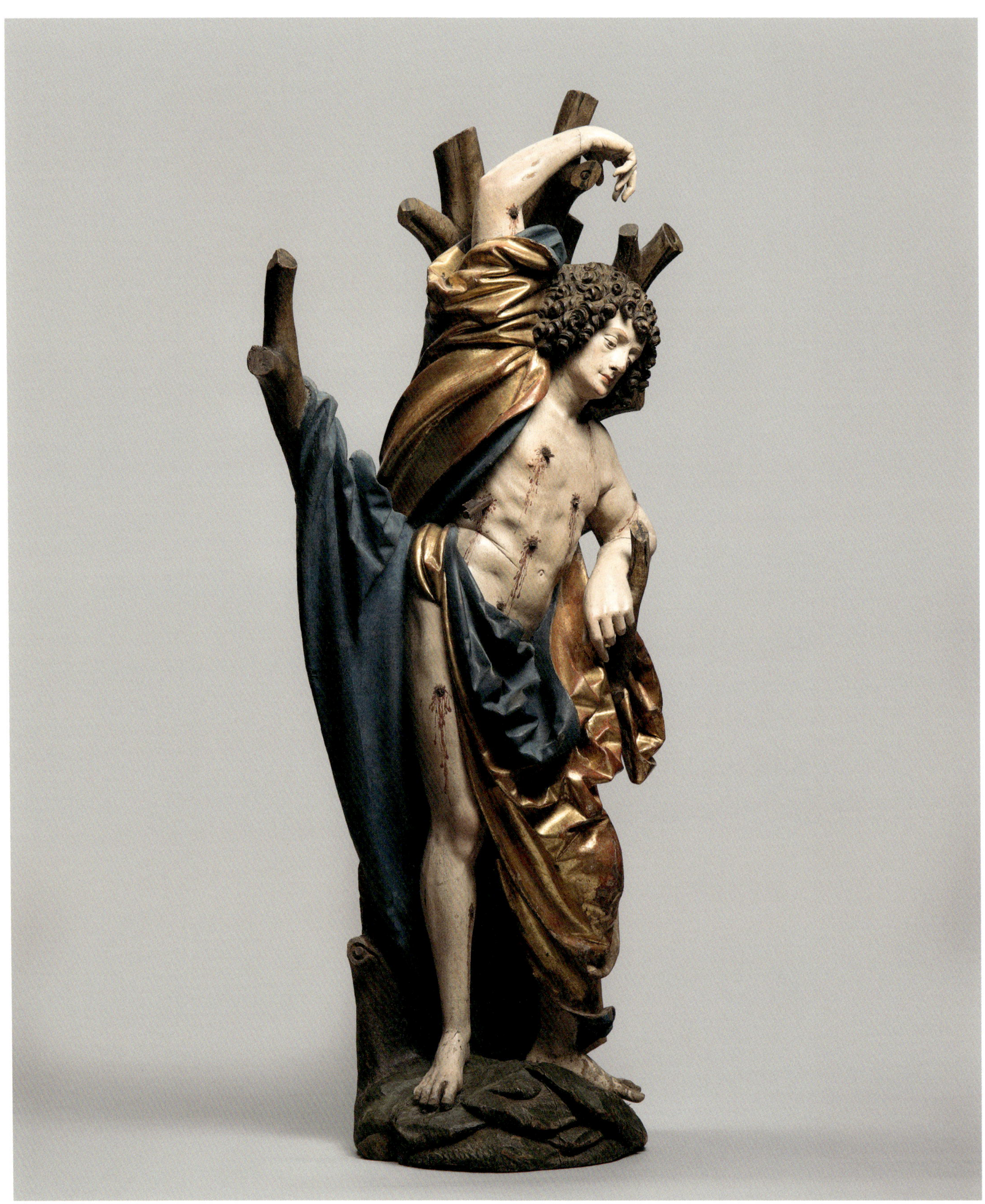

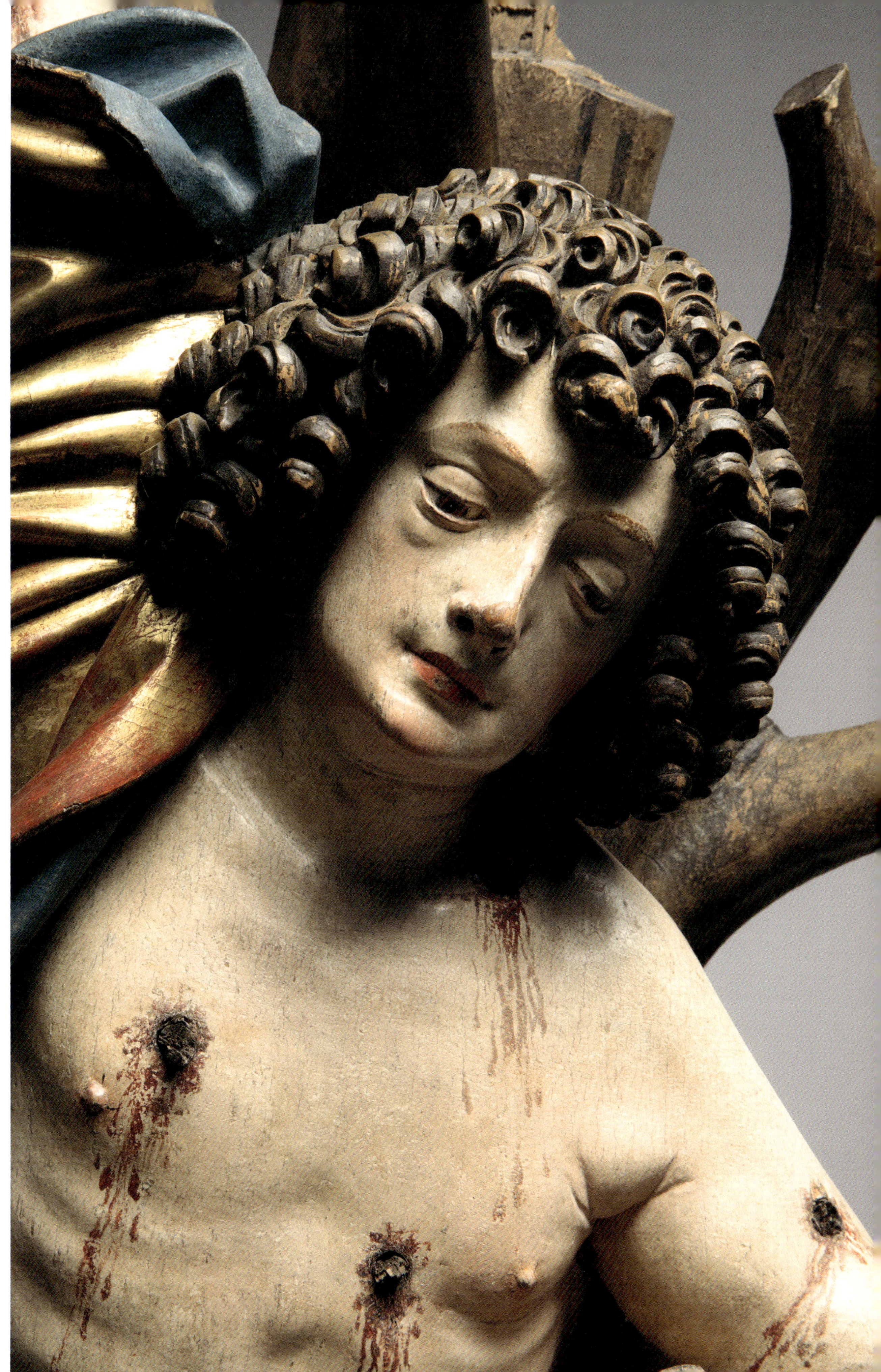

25 Architectural monstrance with two saints

Spain, Barcelona

*c.*1520–1530

63 × 30 × 20.5cm / 24.8 × 11.8 × 8 in.

Gilded silver

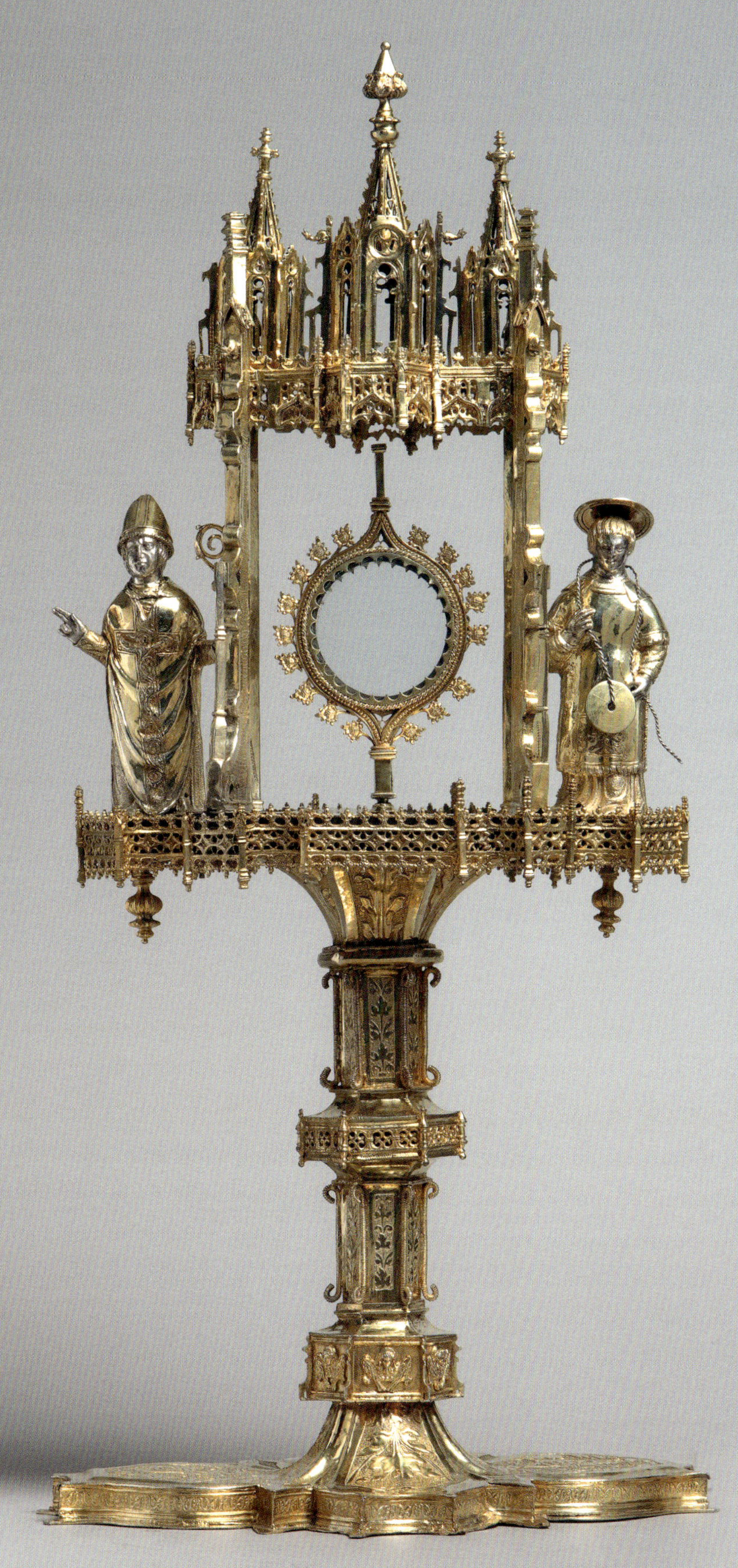

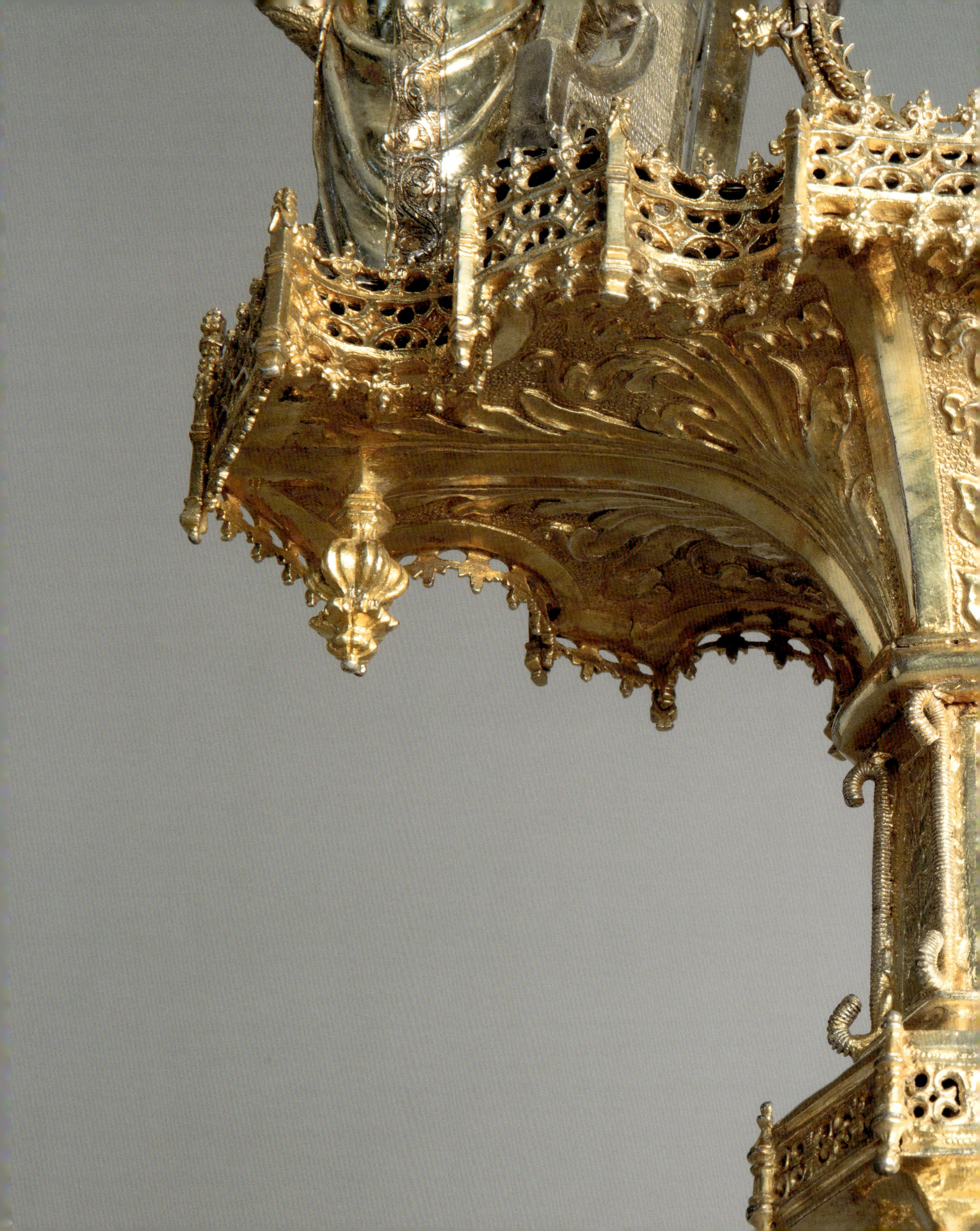

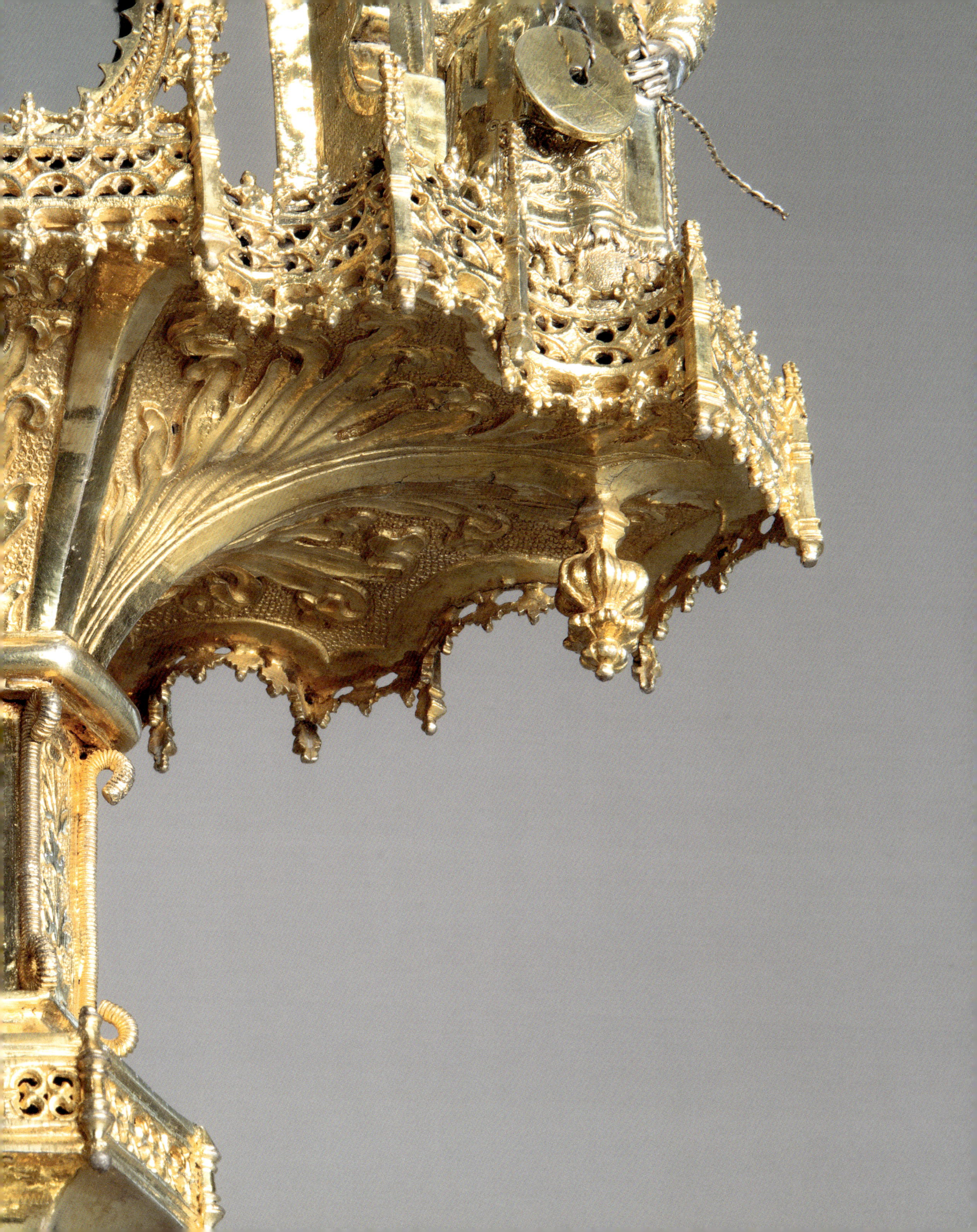

26

Crucified Christ
Germany, Upper Rhine
*c.*1500–1520
115 × 84 × 71 cm / 45 × 33 × 28 in.
Polychromy and gilding on wood

PROVENANCE
Private Collection

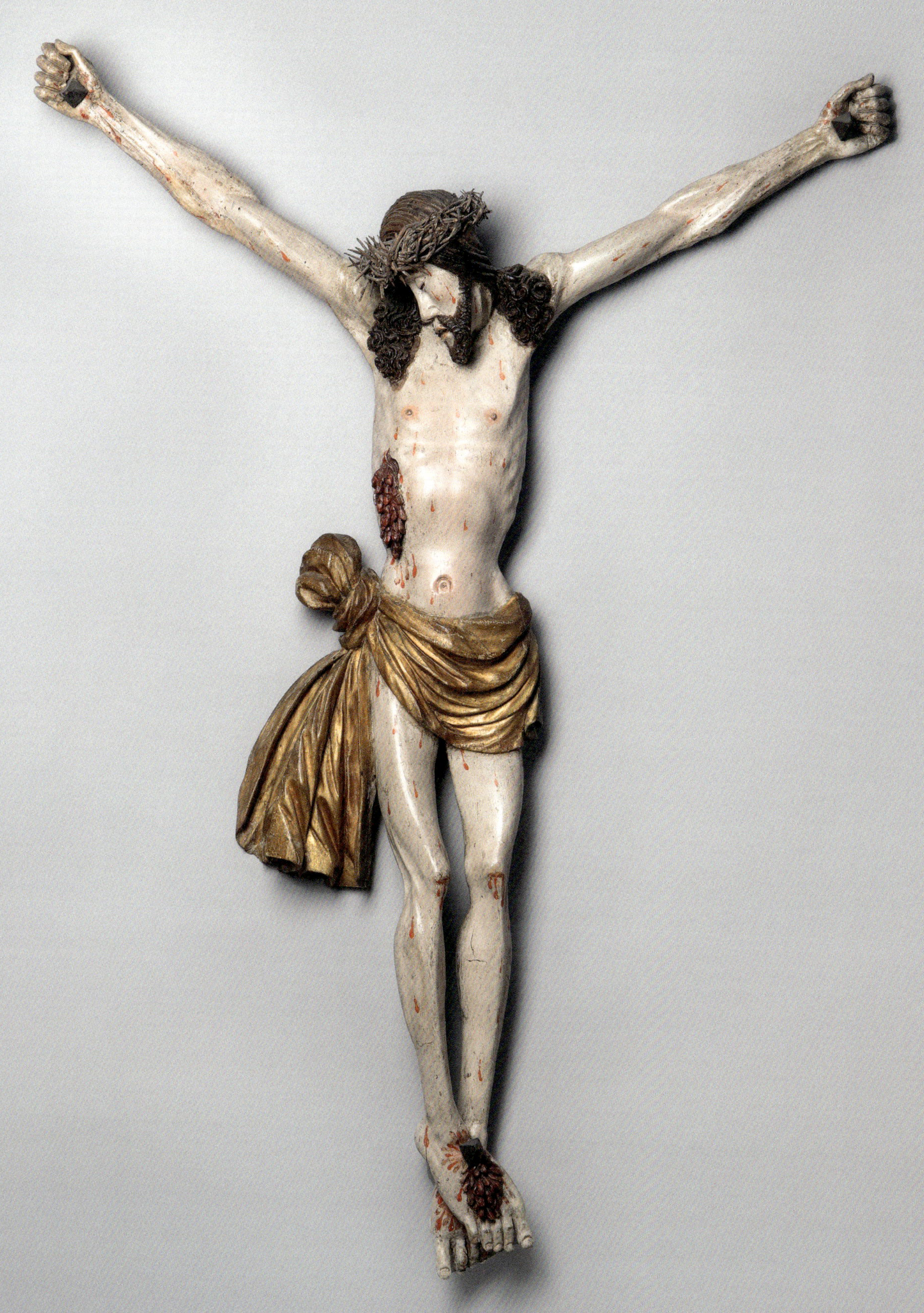

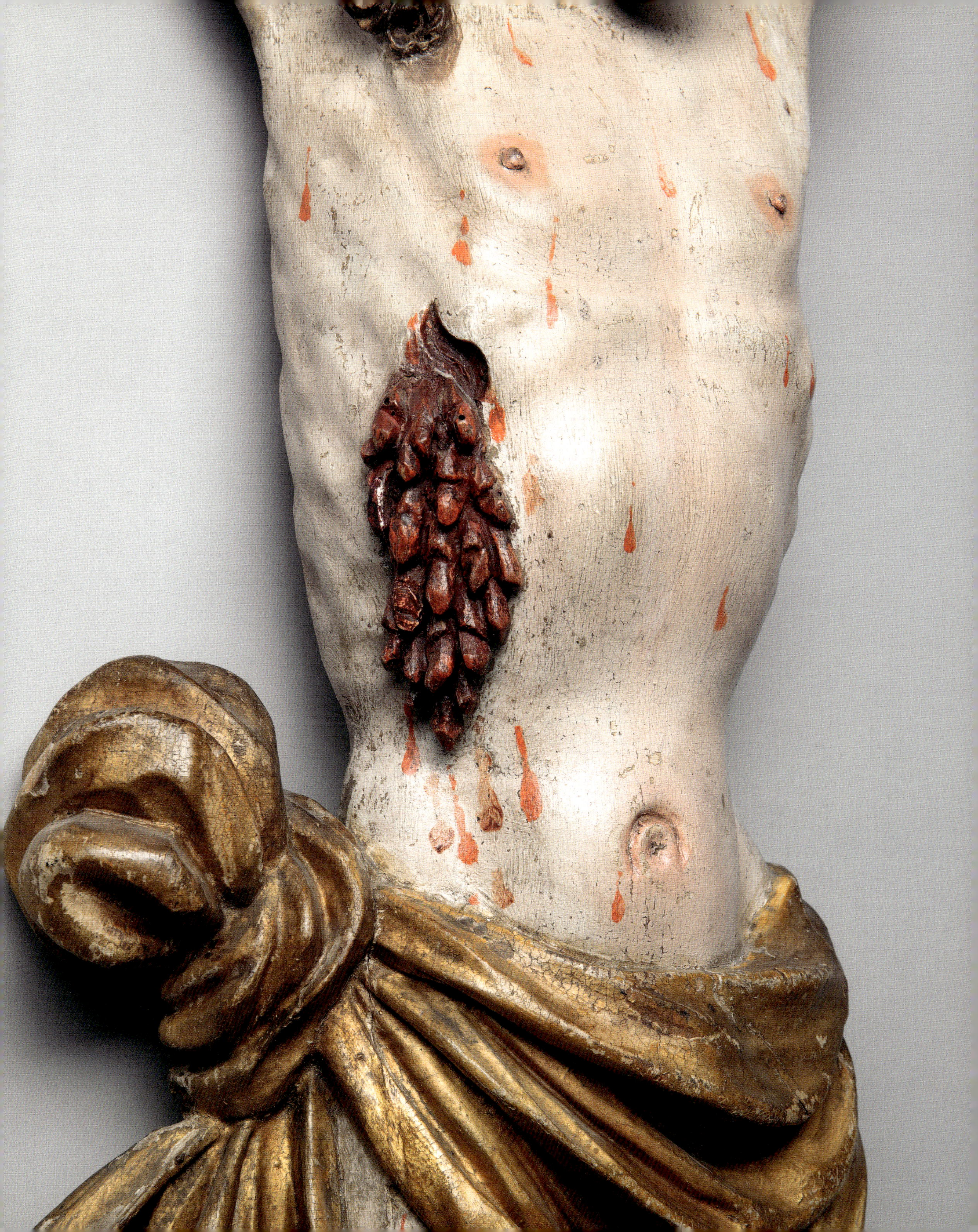

27 **GIOVANNI DELLA ROBBIA** (1469–1529)
Judith holding the head of Holofernes
Italy, Florence
c.1520
62 × 25 × 17 cm / 24.4 × 9.8 × 6.7 in.
Tin-glazed terracotta, inscribed on its socle 'Giuditta ebrea'

PROVENANCE
Collection of Margarete Oppenheim (1857–1935), sold through Julius
Böhler, Munich, 18–22 May 1936; William Randolph Hearst (1863–
1951), acquired at the above sale; Restituted to the Oppenheim family
in 2017; Private Collection, Stuttgart.

PUBLISHED
Böhler (1936), no. 722, fig. 47 ; Seysenegg (1986), page 27–36, no. 114.

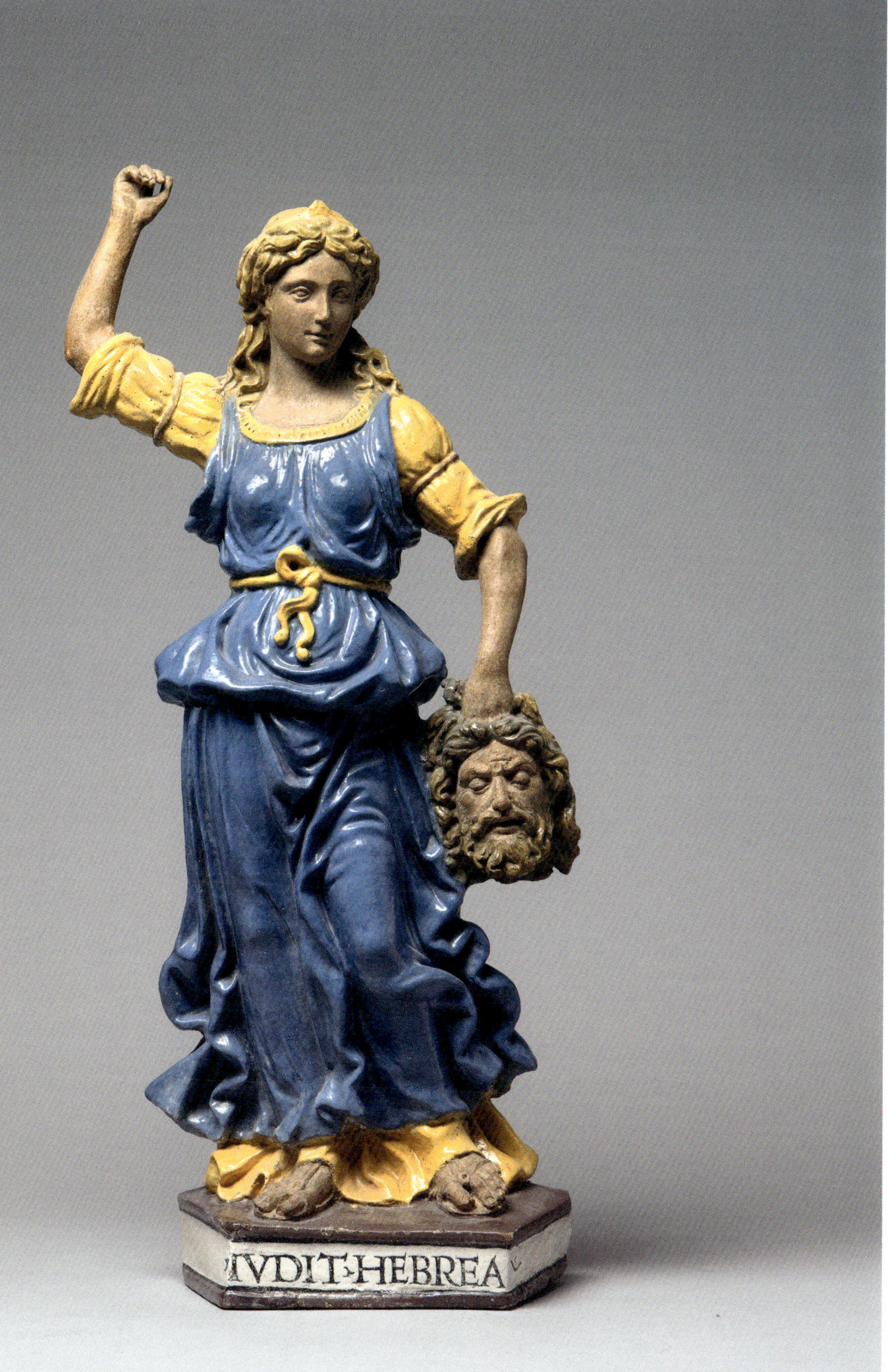

IVDIT·HEBREA

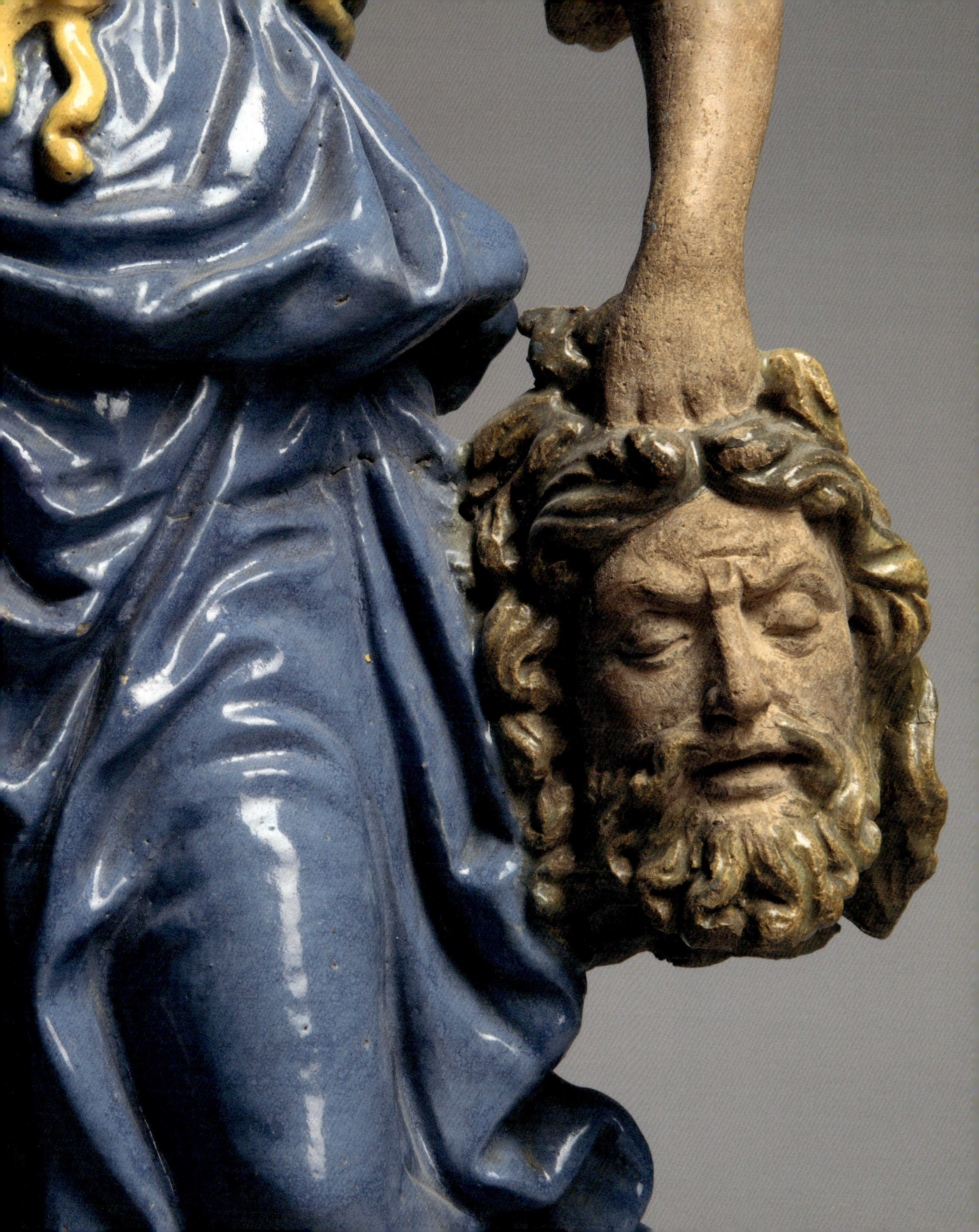

28   **GIOVANNI DA NOLA** (1478–1559)
Effigy of Riccardo Rota (d. 1392)
Italy, Naples, Rota Chapel in San
Domenico Maggiore
*c.*1540–1550
129 × 60 × 43 cm / 50.8 × 23.6 × 17 in.
Marble

PROVENANCE
Sotheby's London 7 December 1995, lot 74;
Private Collection.

EXHIBITED
Tel Aviv Museum of Art, July 1997–
December 2019

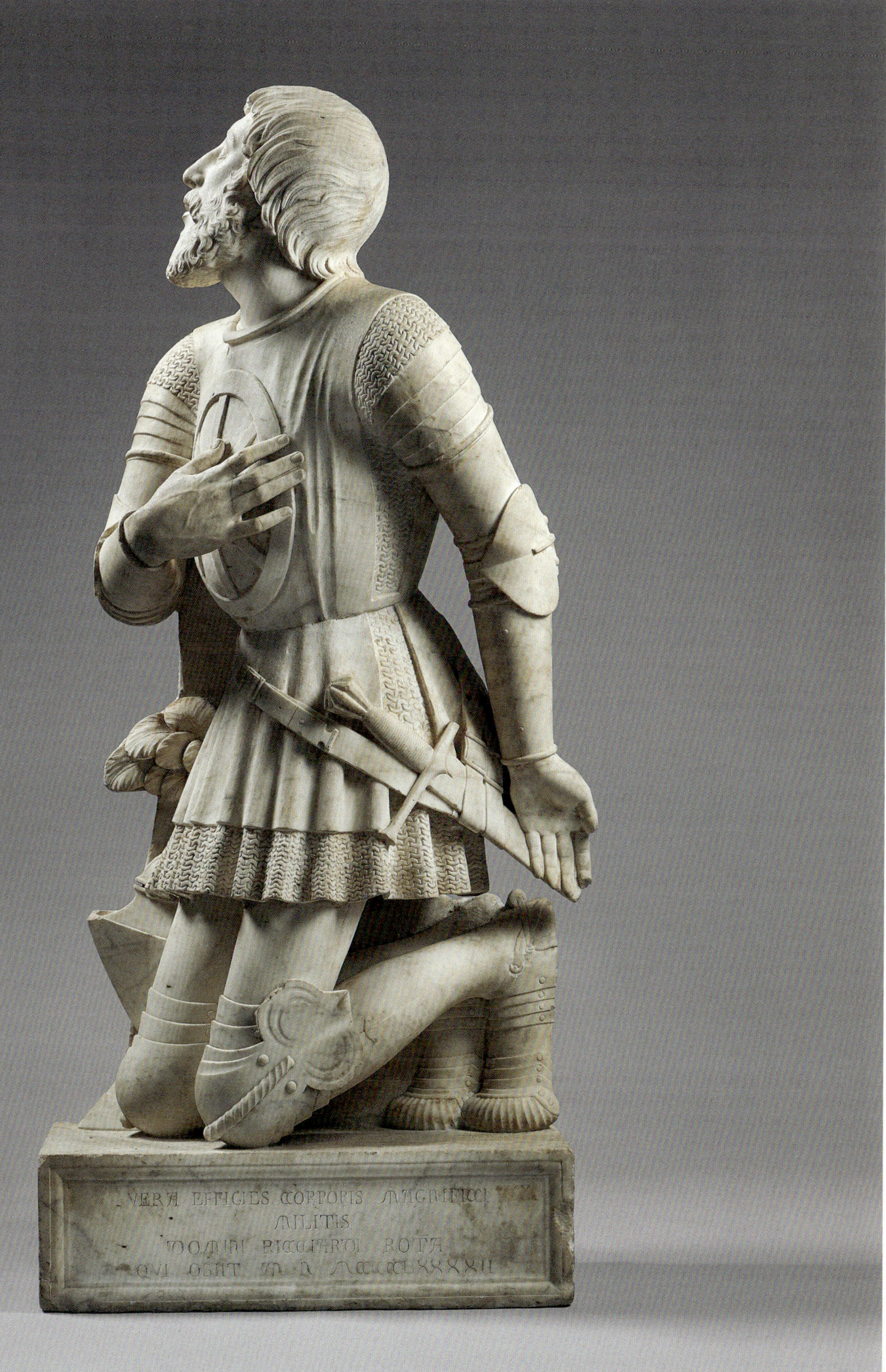
VERA EFFIGIES CORPORIS MAGNIFICI
MILITIS
DOMINI RICCIARDI ROTA
QVI OBIIT M D MCCCCLXXXXII

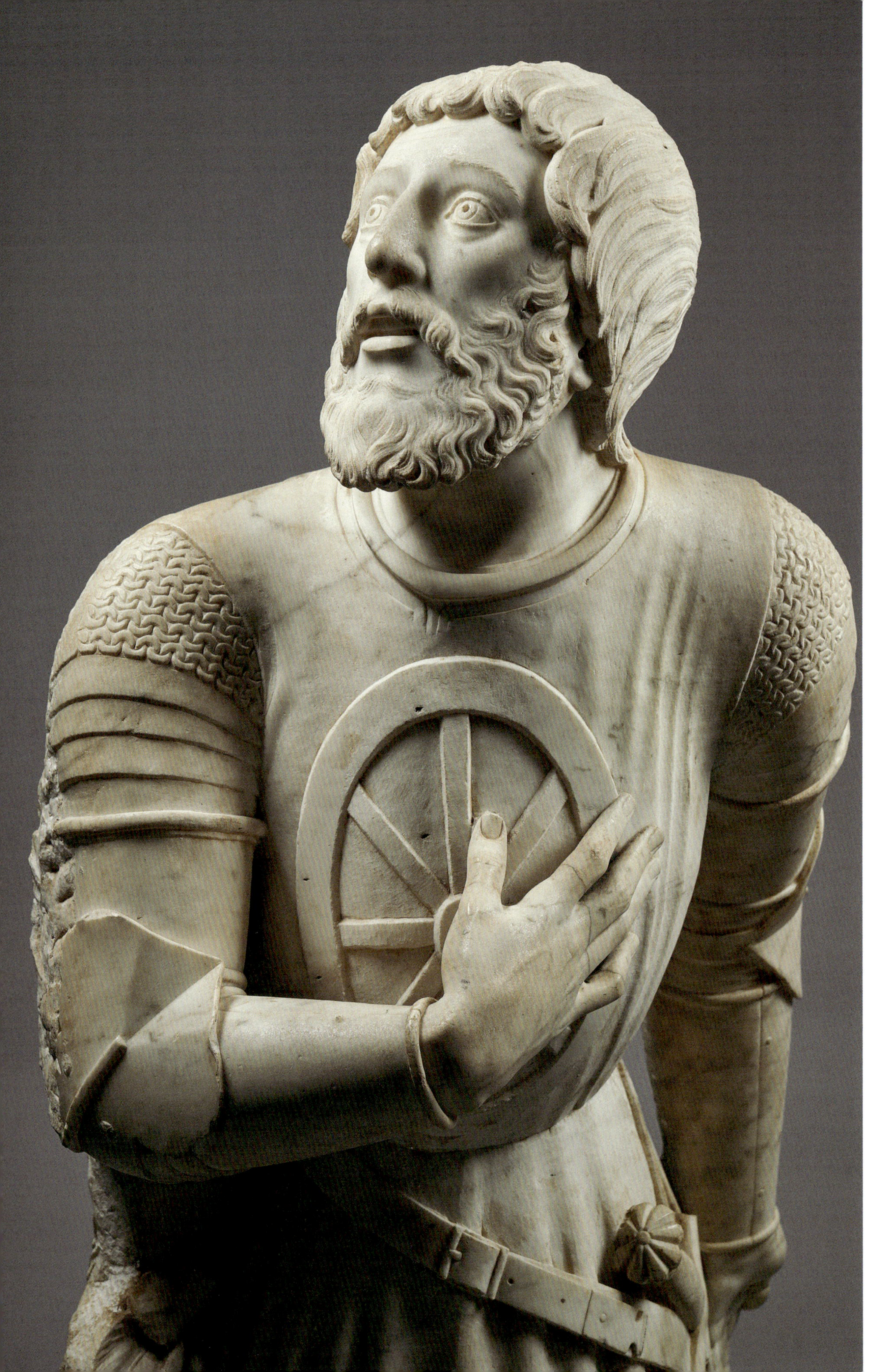

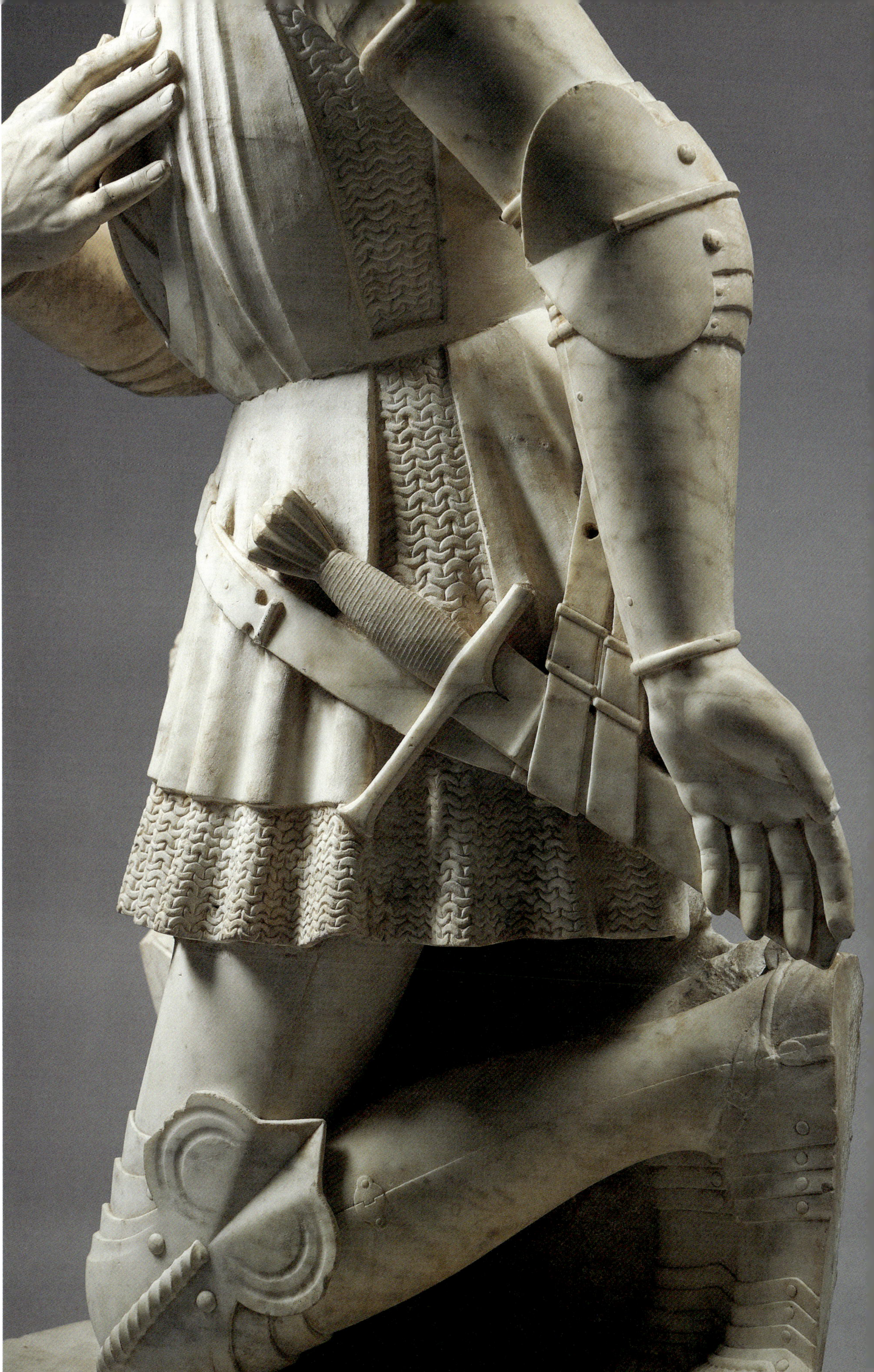

29

The Pozzi Gospels
*Painted and decorated by the artist
Hakob Jughayets'i (c.1550–1613)*
Armenia, Keghi
Dated 1586
19.7 × 14.4 cm/ 7.8 × 5.7 in.
Paper with blind-stamped brown leather
binding; 403 folios; with 46 full-page
illuminations and numerous marginal
miniatures

PROVENANCE
Collection of Jean Pozzi (1884–1967), Paris

PUBLISHED
Greenwood and Vardanyan (2006).

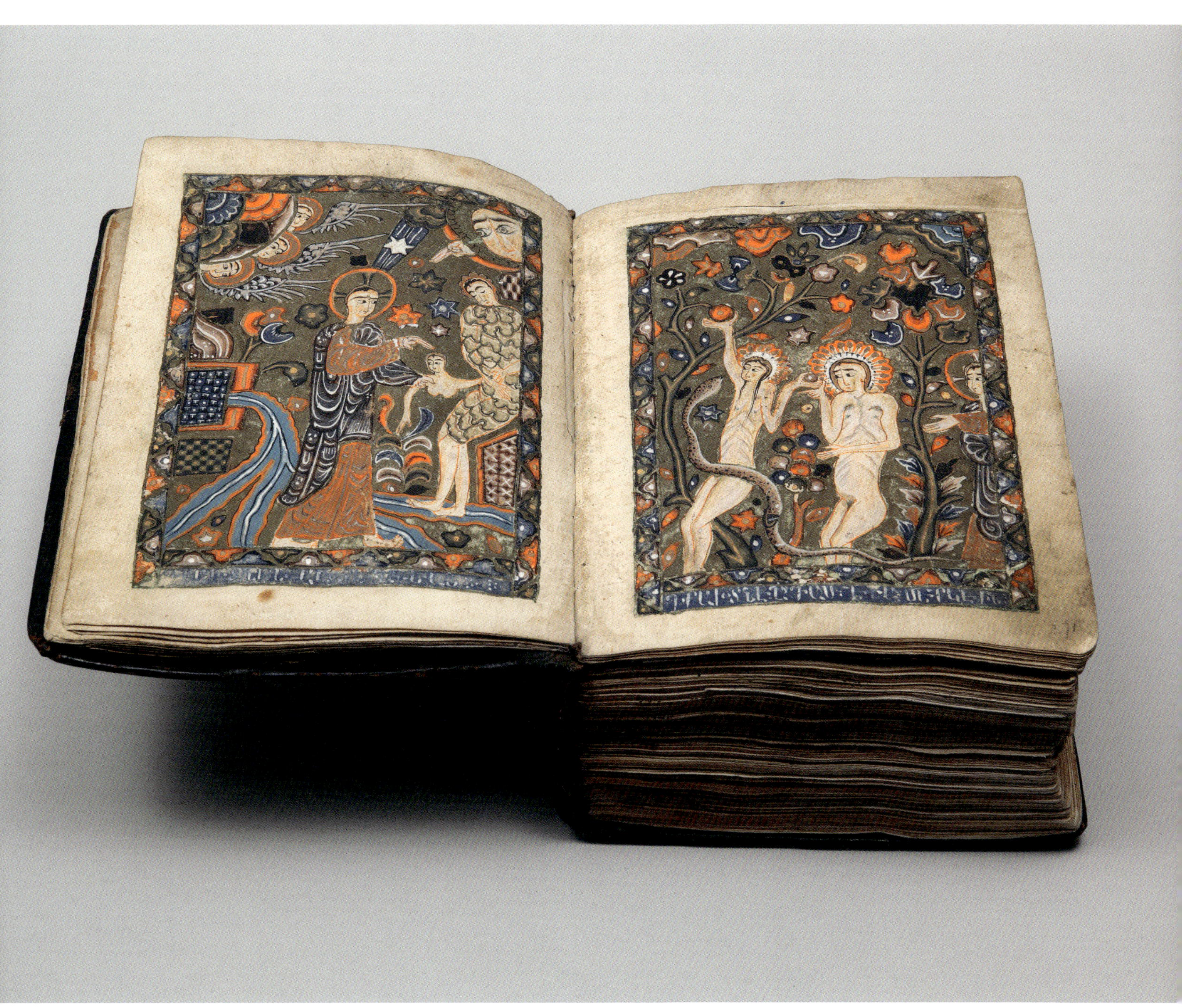

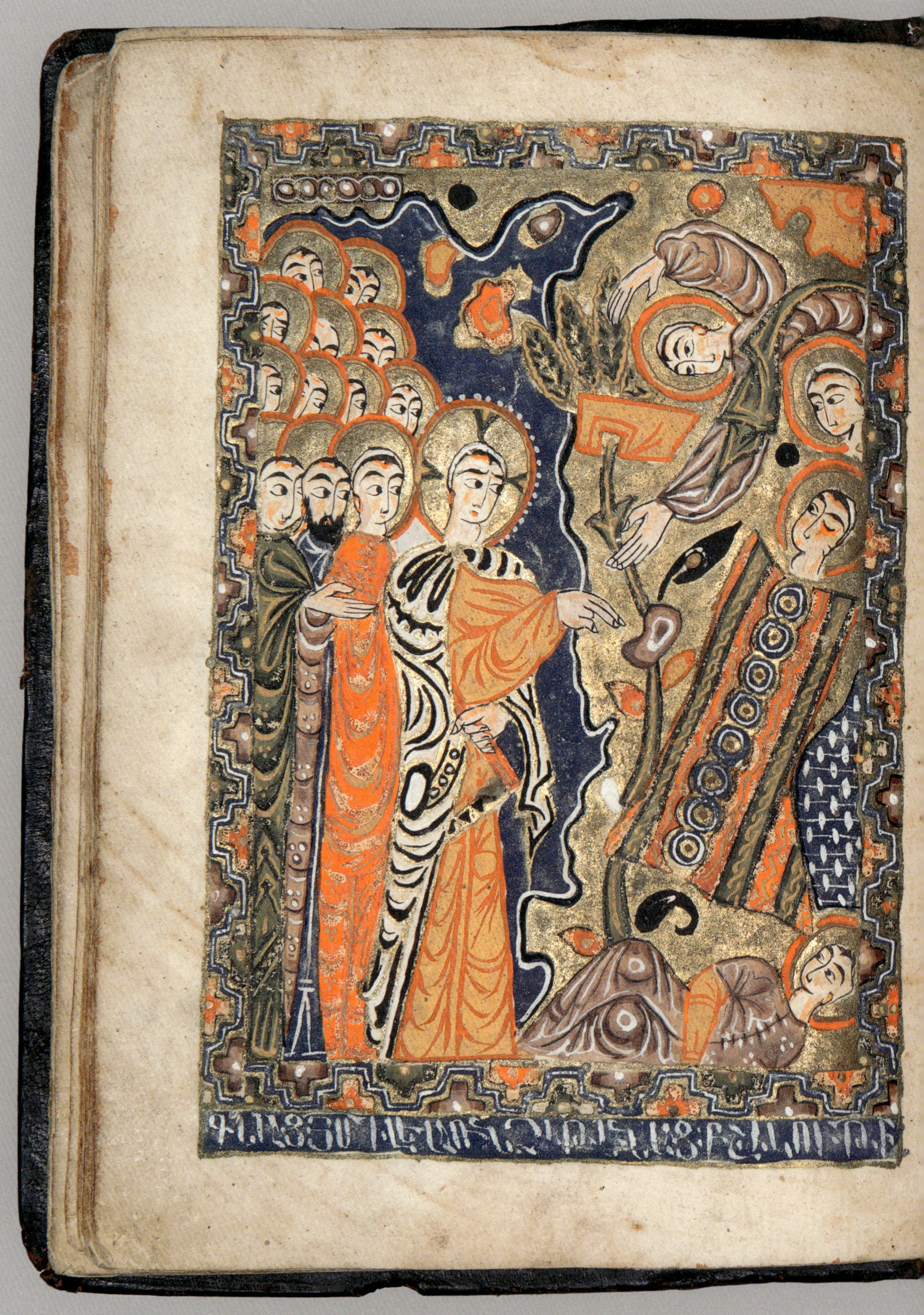

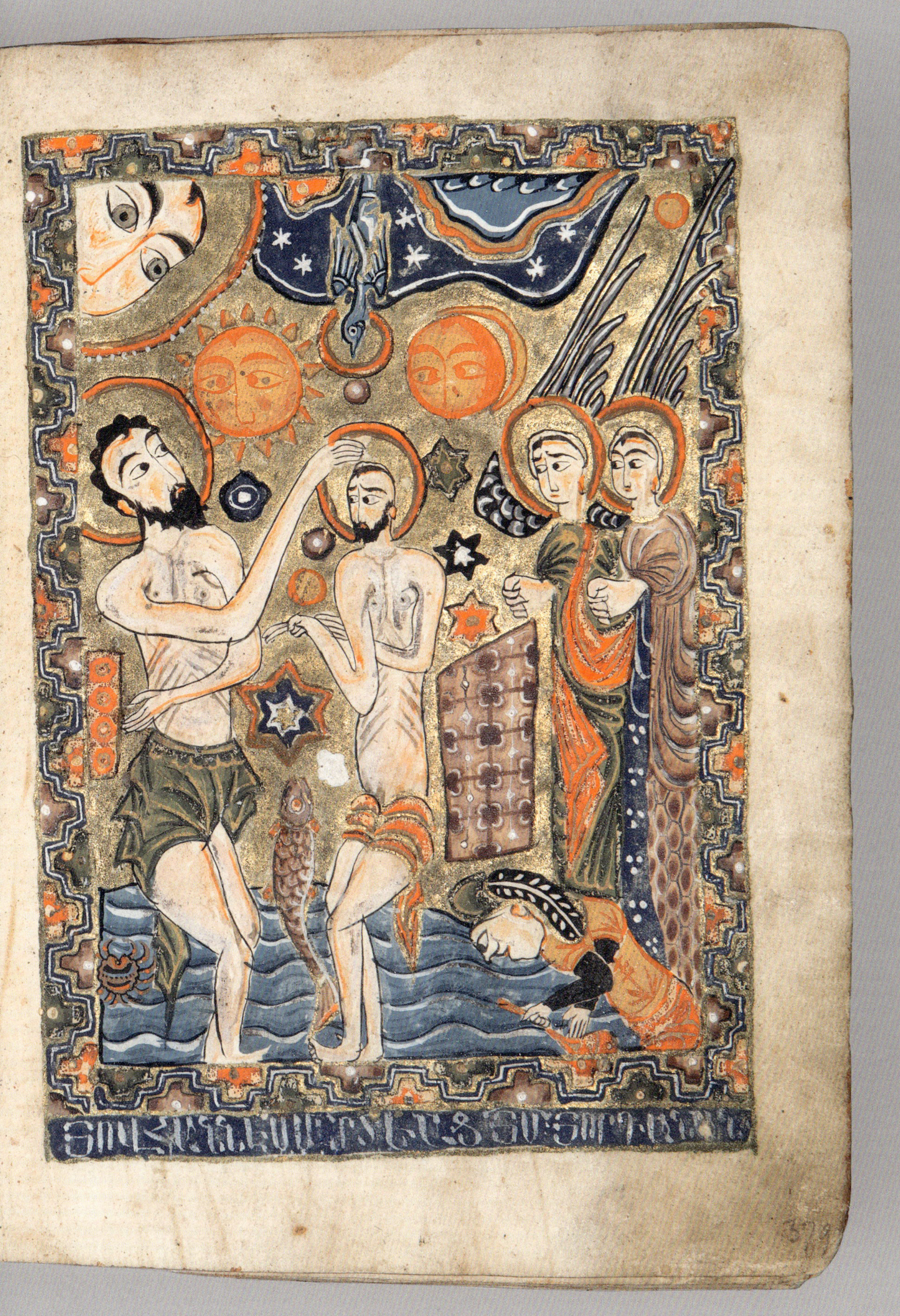

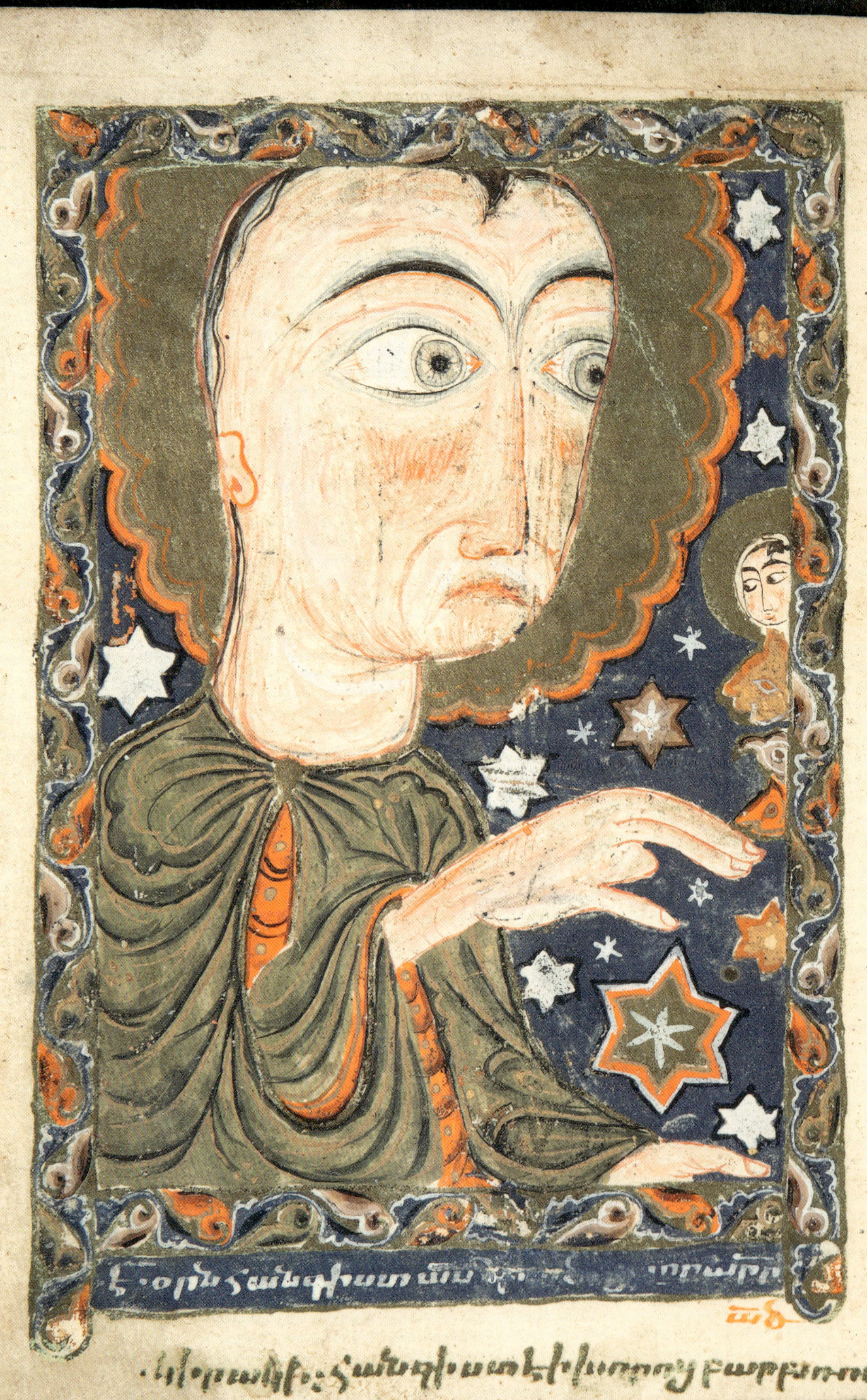

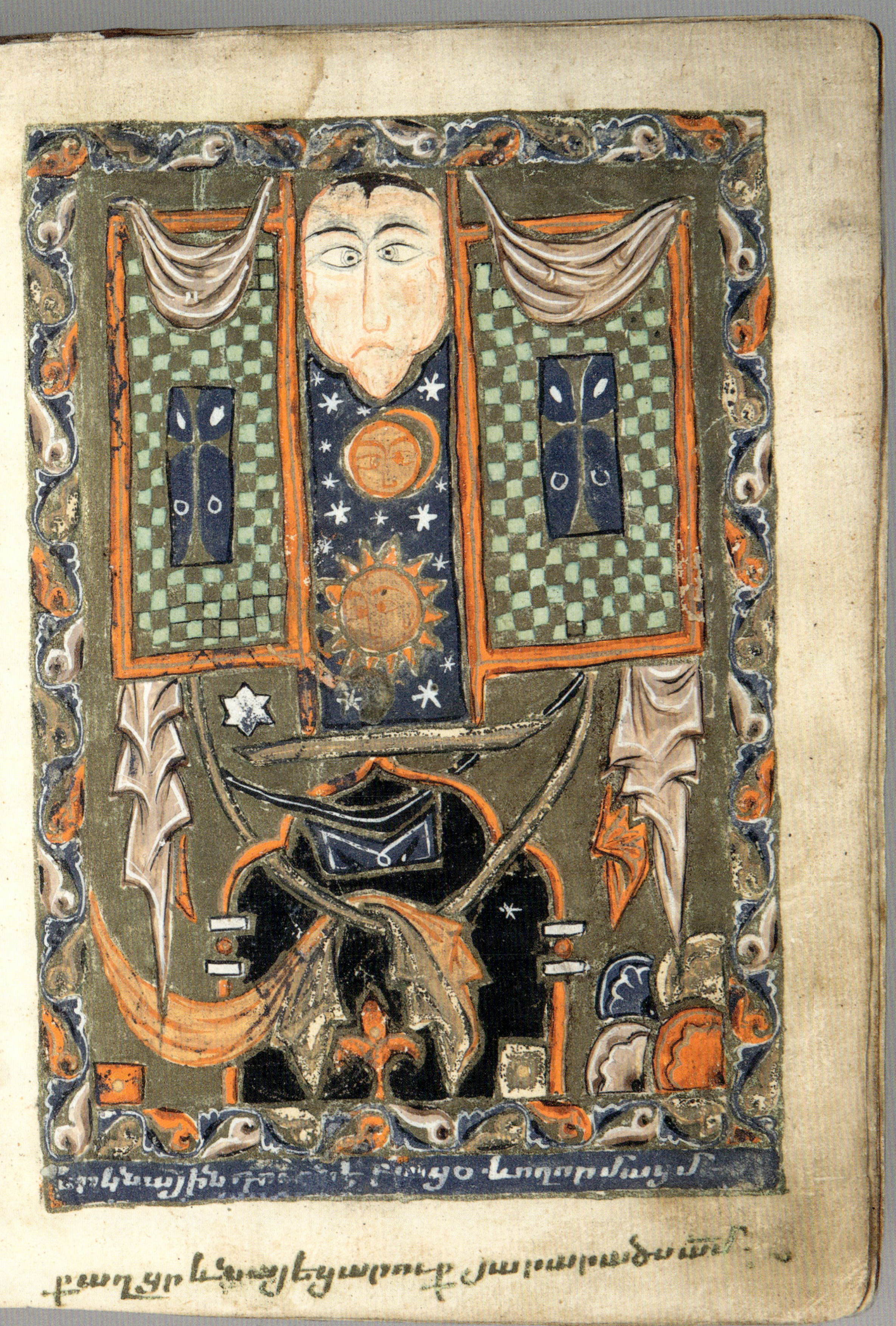
Ի Քրիստոս Աստուծոյ

BIBLIOGRAPHY

Alfred Jones, E. *Catalogue of the Plate belonging to the Duke of Portland, K.G., G.C.V.O. at Welbeck Abbey*, London, 1935.

Art in the Dark Ages in Europe, c.400–1000 A.D. Catalogue of an Exhibition held at the Burlington Fine Arts Club, London. Oxford and London, 1930.

Beal P. and Griffiths, J. eds. *English Manuscript Studies 1100–1700*. Vol. 3, London 1992.

Bellanger, G. and Seillier, C. *Répertoire des cimitieres mérovingiens du Pas-de-Calais*, Bull. Comm. Dép Hist. Arch. Arras, 1982.

Boccador, J. *Statuaire Médiévale en France de 1400 à 1530*. Vol. 1, Zoug, 1974.

Böhler, J. *Sammlung Frau Margarette Oppenheim*. Munich, 23 April–15 May 1936.

Bovey, A. *The Chaworth Roll: A Fourteenth-Century Genealogy of the Kings of England*. London, 2005.

Chapuis, J. *Stefan Lochner: Image Making in Fifteenth-Century Cologne*. Turnhout, 2004.

Coche de la Ferté, E. *Antique Jewellery from the second to the eighth century A.D.*, Hallwag, 1962.

Drivel, E. van. *L'Exposition de Lille: études sur les objets d'art religieux ieunis à Lille en 1874*. Arras, 1876.

Froehner, W. *Collection de la comtesse R. De Béarn*. Paris, 1905.

Godwin, E. W. 'A Very Curious Genealogical Roll of the Kings of England.' In *Proceedings of the Society of Antiquaries of London*, 2nd Series, X, 1883–85.

Greenwood, T. and Vardanyan, E. *Hakob's Gospels. The Life and Work of an Armenian Artist of the Sixteenth Century*. London, 2006.

Griffiths, J. 'Manuscripts in the Schøyen Collection Copied or Owned in the British Isles before 1700.' In *English Manuscript Studies 1100–1700*, eds. Peter Beal and Jeremy Griffiths, 5, London, 1995.

Harcourt House Inventory, 1854.

Husband, T., Blumka, T. and Combs, M. *A Newly Discovered Work by Jörg Lederer: St. Sebastian*. New York, 2017.

Kidd, P. *The McCarthy Collection: French Miniatures*. London, 2021.

Kidd, P. *The McCarthy Collection, Vol. II: Spanish, English, Flemish and Central European Miniatures*, London, 2019.

Laborderie, O. 'Les généalogies des rois d'Angleterre sur rouleaux manuscrits (milieu XIIIe siècle): Conception, diffusion et fonctions.' In *La généalogie entre science et passion*, ed. Tiphaine Barthelemy and Marie-Claude Pingaud, Paris, 1997.

Laborderie, O. 'The First Manuals of English History: Two Late Thirteenth-century Genealogical Rolls of the Kings of England in the Royal Collection.' In *The Electronic British Library Journal* 4, 2014.

Maroto, P. S. 'Un nuevo tríptico de Fernando Gallego.' *Ars Magazine* No. 47, July, 2020.

Peter Beal and Jeremy Griffiths, eds, *English Manuscript Studies 1100–1700*, Vol. 3, London 1992

Pieper. P. 'Zum Werd des Meisters der hl. Veronika.' In *Festschrift für Gert von der Osten*, Cologne, 1970.

Rhein und Maas. Exh. Cat., Cologne, 1972.

Rupp, H. *Die Herkunft der Zelleneinlage und die Almandinscheibenfibeln im Rheinland*, Rheinische Forschungen zur Vorgeschichte, Band 2. Bonn, 1937.

Seysenegg, T. von. 'Die Judith von Giovanni della Robbia.' In *Keramos*, October, 1986.

Stange, A. *Die deutsche Tafelbilder vor Dürer*, I, Munich, No. 44, 1967.

Theuerkauff-Liederwald, A. *Mittelalterliche Bronze- und Messinggefässe: Eimer, Kannen, Lavabokessel*. Berlin, 1988.

Steyaert, J. *Late Gothic Sculpture: The Burgundian Netherlands*, Exh. Cat. Ghent, 1994.

Venturi, A. *La galleria Sterbini in Roma: saggio illustrative*. Roma: Casa editrice de L'Arte. 1906.

Zehnder, F. G. *Katalog der Altkölner Malerei*, Cologne, 1990.

Zehnder, F. G. *Stefan Lochner Meister zu Köln*. Cologne, 1993.

Zeri, F. *Diari di lavoro 2*. Torino 1976.